Function, Selection, and Innateness

'This is an important contribution to linguistics, and one that will be of interest to linguists of all theoretical persuasions to those in virtually all subfields. There are very few other books out that treat issues of form and function in linguistics as thoroughly and as even-handedly as this one.'

Frederick J. Newmeyer, University of Washington

'A brilliant, innovative, computer-simulated exploration into the problem of linkage—a missing link in the current functional attempts at explaining language universals: how functional pressures grammaticalise and become innate properties governing human language and its acquisition. In these short, but richly illustrated pages, Simon Kirby succeeds admirably in integrating usage-based functional approaches and formal, innatist theories. This intelligent, thought-provoking book is an essential reading for all those concerned with grammatical theory—functional or formal, language universals, linguistic typology and historical change.'

Professor Masayoshi Shibatani, Kobe University

'In this important and highly original work Simon Kirby proposes a new method for addressing a major issue in the explanation of language universals. If many universals are to be explained by processing efficiency, then how do the preferences of performance actually become the fixed, and variant, conventions of grammars that we observe in current language samples? Kirby's computer simulations model the "adaptive mechanism", and his discussion of the relationship between function, selection and innateness is both clarifying and timely.'

Jon A. Hawkins, Department of Linguistics,
University of Southern California

Function, Selection, and Innateness

The Emergence of Language Universals

SIMON KIRBY

OXFORD
UNIVERSITY PRESS

OXFORD
UNIVERSITY PRESS

Great Clarendon Street, Oxford OX2 6DP
Oxford New York

Athens Auckland Bangkok Bogotá Buenos Aires Calcutta
Cape Town Chennai Dar es Salaam Delhi Florence Hong Kong Istanbul
Karachi Kuala Lumpur Madrid Melbourne Mexico City Mumbai
Nairobi Paris São Paulo Singapore Taipei Tokyo Toronto Warsaw
and associated companies in Berlin Ibadan

Oxford is a registered trade mark of Oxford University Press

Published in the United States
by Oxford University Press, Inc., New York

British Library Cataloging in Publication Data
Data available

Library of Congress Cataloging in Publication Data
Function, selection, and innateness: the emergence of
language universals/Simon Kirby.
Includes bibliographical references and index.
1. Universals (Linguistics) 2. Language and languages–Philosophy.
3. Linguistics–Methodology. 4. Functionalism (Linguistics)
5. Innateness hypothesis (Linguistics) I. Title.
P204.K53   1999   401–dc21   98-37704 CIP
ISBN 0-19-823812-6 (pbk.)
ISBN 19-823811-8
10 9 8 7 6 5 4 3 2 1

Typeset by Newgen Imaging Systems (P) Ltd., Chennai, India
Printed in Great Britain on acid-free paper by
Biddles Ltd., Guildford and King's Lynn

For my Dad,

who can explain more on the back of a napkin
than I can in all these pages.

Preface

At the core of modern linguistics and cognitive science are a number of questions so basic that they are rarely made explicit in the literature:

- How much of human language can be understood by looking at the way it is used?
- Do some aspects of language have their own internal logic which *cannot* be explained by looking at the way language is used?
- Why is it that all languages are similar in some highly specific ways, but in other ways seem completely different?
- How is it that languages appear to be partially stable over time and space, but are also liable to change?
- How did humans evolve the capacity to learn language, and how might an understanding of the evolution of the language faculty affect our understanding of language?

Much of the literature on communication, generative grammar, typology, language change and variation, and primate evolution illuminates our understanding of individual questions in this list by looking in detail at certain aspects of human language. However, the answers to these questions interact with each other in complex ways, and it is often hard to see how the various fields' approaches can be reconciled.

This book takes a look at these problems from a broad perspective, with the intention of showing that these questions can (indeed, must) be studied together. I take, as my starting point, two apparently opposed approaches to explaining universal properties of language. The functionalist tradition in linguistics argues that the constraints on variation from language to language are due to the communicative use of language. The other influential approach, often known as formalism, highlights instead the internal structure of language as a formal system. The formalist approach claims that language universals can be explained by an innate (and therefore universally shared) language faculty in humans.

I claim not only that these two major approaches to linguistics can be unified, but also that full explanatory adequacy can be achieved only by doing so. I put forward a view of language universals as *emergent* from a constantly repeating cycle of language use and acquisition, where local actions of the individual users of language conspire to produce non-local, universal patterns of variation. This is an approach that treats language as a whole as an *adaptive system*. The communicative aspects of language and the formal aspects of language have crucial and complementary roles in the description of this system.

The main problem with understanding language universals as emergent properties is that in order to discover which properties emerge from which assumptions we need to model the behaviour of populations of individuals over time. The very nature of emergence is such that the global behaviour of a system cannot simply be read from the local behaviour.

A solution to this problem lies in the use of computational simulations which allow us to build working models of linguistic populations. These models can show what universals emerge given a particular theory about language use and/or acquisition. This is the methodology I have developed in this book. I believe it to be both a useful way of explicitly testing explanations for language universals, and a powerful demonstration of the relevance of looking at language as an adaptive system.

This book is a somewhat modified version of my postgraduate thesis, on which I worked at the Department of Linguistics in the University of Edinburgh. Further work on the manuscript was completed while at the Collegium Budapest Institute for Advanced Study and later at the Language Evolution and Computation Research Unit again at the Department of Linguistics in Edinburgh.

Before I started writing up, I was under the impression that it would be an extremely painful activity. I am glad to say that, surprisingly, this was not the case. However, I feel sure that this was largely due to the assistance and generosity of those around me (some of whom would probably disagree with me on how painless the whole thing was!).

First, my greatest thanks go to my supervisor and colleague, Jim Hurford, whose patience with my continual requests and readiness to engage in impromptu supervisions at random times when I was a postgraduate student kept my interest and excitement in the subject alive. Also to Diane Nelson, who supported me through every stage and all aspects of this book's preparation—Di, you are on every page.

The manuscript went through the transformation from thesis to book thanks mainly to the patient help of two editors from Oxford University Press: Frances Morphy and John Davey.

Several linguists have read and commented on this manuscript in full at various stages, so a large round of drinks to: Jack Hawkins, Caroline Heycock, Fritz Newmeyer (whose extensive and thoughtful comments have shaped much of the final volume), Bernard Comrie, and two anonymous reviewers.

Thanks are also due to the many people who have taken time to comment on my work, send me papers, or otherwise assist and give encouragement. In particular: Bob Berwick, Ted Briscoe, Ronnie Cann, Robert Clark, Daniel Wedgwood, Mike Oliphant, Catriona MacPherson, and Louise Kelly. Not all of these people will agree with what I have said, of course, and none of them is responsible for any mistakes.

The research for and preparation of this book was made possible in part because of the quality of the software that was used, almost all of which was produced for free in the spirit of GNU and Linux. The many people who work on these projects are amassing a great debt of gratitude.

A large part of what has made my research so enjoyable is down to the nature of the Department of Linguistics in Edinburgh. Thanks to those that keep it from falling apart around us, especially Ethel Jack, Irene McLeod, Eddie Dubourg, and Cedric MacMartin (again, for incredible patience).

Finally, general feelings of love and gratitude go out to Helen Weetman, Ian Hodson, Paul Gilbody, Dave Patterson, The Ugly Groove Movement, Anna Claybourne, and my parents.

S.K.

Edinburgh
1998

Contents

List of Figures

List of Tables

Abbreviations

AH	accessibility hierarchy
ASP	aspect
Adj	adjective
BDT	branching direction theory
C′	complementizer-bar
CP	complementizer-phrase
CRD	constituent recognition domain
Comp	complementizer
D	determiner
D′	determiner-bar
DO	direct object
DP	determiner phrase
Det	determiner
EIC	early immediate constituent (recognition)
GB	government and binding theory
Gen	genitive
HPSG	head-driven phrase structure grammar
I	indirect object relative
I	inflection
I′	inflection-bar
IC	immediate constituent
IO	indirect object
IP	inflection phrase
LAD	language acquisition device
LF	logical form
MNCC	mother node constructing category
MSG	male-singular
MUT	mutation
Mod	modifier
N	noun
NP	noun phrase

O	object relative
OBL	oblique
OV	verb after object
P	preposition/postposition
PF	phonetic form
PFLP	phonetic form licensing principle
PLD	primary linguistic data
PP	adpositional phrase
Po	postposition(al)
Postp	postposition(al)
Pr	preposition(al)
PrNMH	prepositional noun-modifier hierarchy
Pref	prefix
Prep	preposition(al)
Pron	pronoun
RC	relative clause
Rel	relative
S	sentence
S	subject relative
S'	sentence-bar
SG	singular
SOV	subject–object–verb
SVO	subject–verb–object
Spec	specifier
Suff	suffix
UG	universal grammar
V	verb
VO	verb before object
VP	verb phrase
VSO	verb–subject–object

1 A Puzzle of Fit

A striking feature of the natural world is the existence of organisms whose occurrence is improbable simply by virtue of their complexity.[1] Matter seems to arrange itself into highly organized bundles whenever life intervenes. The examples of this improbable order extend to the artefacts of life as well as to living things themselves: for example, the buildings, roads, and pavements that make up towns and, more abstractly, the cultural patterns that give rise to these artefacts. All these things are improbable in the sense that they inhabit a small, organized area in the much larger space of logical possibility.

This book looks at another phenomenon in the natural world: human language. The range of variation among languages is constrained in various interesting ways. 'Language universals' are statements which describe these constraints on variation. These universals map the boundaries of a small area in the space of logically possible languages, within which the actual languages of the world are found. In other words, languages do not randomly vary from instance to instance, but rather embody a kind of pattern and ordered complexity similar to that found in life and its other artefacts.

The origin of this order is in itself interesting, but I shall be exploring a particular aspect of these constraints on variation which are shared by others in the natural world. This aspect can be termed 'fit' or 'the appearance of design'. For example, trees appear to be designed for the purpose of surviving in the world and producing more trees—looking deeper, we can say they appear to be designed for converting carbon dioxide and sunlight into more tree, and so on. Buildings appear to be designed efficiently to contain people and their possessions without harm from the weather (in fact, we know they are designed for this purpose). As Cziko (1995) (from whom this chapter title is borrowed) points out, this 'fit' of form to function pervades the world of living organisms and their products.

As we shall see, this appearance of design is also a striking feature of language universals. Many attempts at explaining universals have pointed out the fit of these constraints of variation to the functions of language. Although these observations are important and insightful, I believe they

---

[1] No definition of this type of complexity is given here. Algorithmic complexity is not a good definition, since some organized, complex distributions (e.g. fractal sets) can be defined quite simply. See e.g. Gell-Mann 1992 for some discussion.

leave the real mystery unsolved. Rather than explaining the origin of universals, this fit is itself a puzzle. Where does it come from, and what mechanisms can explain how it arises? A careful study of this question casts light on many issues in modern linguistics and reflects back on the various views of what makes a 'possible human language'.

Constraints on variation

I have mentioned that language universals can be thought of as mapping the constraints of variation on occurring languages in some more general space of logically possible languages. Figure 1.1 demonstrates how this works. In Figure 1.1*a*, the occurring languages (shown in grey) are evenly spread throughout the space of all logically possible languages (the whole space, labelled 'E', as is the convention with Venn diagrams). If this were the case, then there would be very little of interest that we could say about constraints on variation. In some sense, there would be nothing *cross-linguistic* to explain about languages. All we could hope to do is explain how *one particular language* happened to come to be in a particular point in the space 'E'.

However, as previously mentioned, languages do not vary randomly—they do not evenly fill the space of possibility. In other words, the real situation is more like that in Figure 1.1*b*. Here, the languages cluster in a tightly constrained sub-part of the space. The boundary of this grey cluster is completely specified by the set of language universals.

What this cluster will look like and where it will be in diagrams such as these will depend on how we organize the space of logically possible languages. It is impossible to draw this space on a flat piece of paper, since it has many dimensions. Instead, typologists choose to look at a small number of dimensions when discussing a particular universal and consider how languages cluster when we draw the space 'E' highlighting only those dimensions.

Figure 1.1*c* shows a very simple example. Here, the space of logically possible languages has been arranged so that it is divided neatly into two types of language: those in which overt subject noun-phrases are possible, and those in which overt subject noun-phrases are impossible. All other dimensions along which languages may vary are ignored. It turns out that all languages allow overt subject noun phrases, so the grey cluster fills the left-hand side of the diagram.

This representation of the space 'E' is enriched in Figure 1.1*d*, where a second orthogonal dimension cuts across the first one. In this diagram, languages at the top of the space are those that do not possess vowels, and

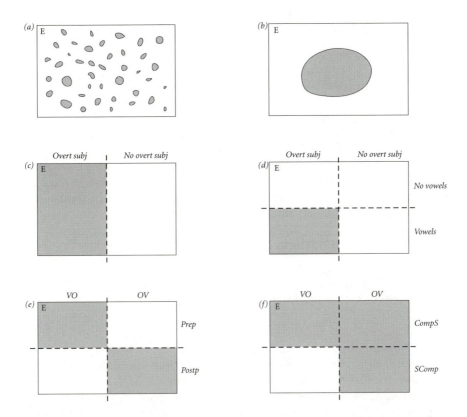

Figure 1.1. Venn diagrams showing various ways in which human languages (in grey) might vary in the space of logically possible languages (E). Refer to the text for details.

languages at the bottom of the space are those that do. Now, because there are no languages that lack vowels, the grey space in the figure is more tightly constrained. In theory typologists could go on adding more dimensions and get closer to a specification of 'what makes a possible human language'.

However, there is something unsatisfying about this approach. Are we not just compiling a list of facts about language that are completely independent of each other? It is more interesting—and begs more explanation—when the orthogonal typological dimensions are actually related to one another in some way. Figure 1.1*e* gives just such an example. The left–right split in the space is between languages that typically order their verb before their object noun phrase (such as English in Example 1.1), and languages that order their object before their verb (such as Japanese in Example 1.2).

(1.1) Everyone loves someone

(1.2) Minna ga dareka o aisiteiru
      all   someone loving
      'Everyone loves someone'   (Shibatani 1990: 261)

Notice that, by giving two example languages, we can see that if this was our only typological dimension we would not be able to say anything at all about constraints on variation: both types occur.

The top–bottom split in the space divides languages with prepositions (preceding the noun phrase they are modifying, such as English in Example 1.3) from languages with postpositions (following the noun phrase they are modifying, such as Japanese in Example 1.4).

(1.3) Dr Heycock is teaching Japanese in the classroom

(1.4) Kakehi sensei ga kyoositu   de eigo o   osie-teiru
          prof.   classroom in English teach-be
      'Prof. Kakehi is teaching English in the classroom'
                                  (Shibatani 1990: 287)

Once again, there are examples of both types of language, so either typological dimension on its own tells us nothing about cross-linguistic distribution. However, if they are put together, as in the figure, then it becomes obvious that these two dimensions are related, in that the verb-before-object (or VO) languages are all prepositional and the verb-after-object (or OV) languages are all postpositional.[2]

There is another significant way in which two typological dimensions can be related. In Figure 1.1*f* the first dimension is the same as in the previous example—in other words, the split between VO and OV. The orthogonal dimension here, however, is the ordering of complementizer (e.g. English *that*) and subordinate clause. We can see that if a language orders its verb before its object then it will order its complementizer before the subordinate clause, as in the English Example 1.5. On the other hand, if a language is OV, then no prediction can reliably be made about the order of its complementizer and subordinate clause. So, whilst Japanese in Example 1.6 has a final complementizer, German (which is OV in subordinate clauses at least) has an initial complementizer in Example 1.7.

---

[2] There are some, though relatively few, exceptions to this generalization. According to Hawkins (1983), out of a sample of 336 languages, 26 are postpositional and VO, and 12 are prepositional and OV.

(1.5) Ken knows that Heather sings the song

(1.6) ken-wa heather-ga sono uta-wo utatta to   itta
       Ken   Heather   that song   sang COMP said
       'Ken said that Heather sang that song'

(1.7) Ken weiss, dass   Heather das Lied singt
       Ken knows COMP Heather the song sings
       'Ken knows that Heather sings the song'

These three languages exemplify points in the top left, bottom right, and top right of the diagram respectively. However, there are no languages that have VO&SComp, which is why the bottom left of the diagram is not filled in.

Forms of constraints

We have looked informally at the ways in which languages may vary in the space of logical possibility, and seen that there are many possible ways we can express the constraints on this variability. The formal expression of these cross-linguistic universals involves two distinct steps:

Typology.   This is a taxonomy which categorizes languages along some dimension on the basis of an identifiable property of the language. For the purposes of formulating a universal, orthogonal typologies may be considered, leading to a particular language being placed in a multi-dimensional space.

Constraints.   The actual universal is stated as a constraint on possible language types, defining a sub-space within the space defined by the typology.

The constraints may take various forms, which can be usefully categorized on two dimensions (notice that the broad distinctions here are recognized by other authors (e.g. Greenberg 1963; Comrie 1981; Hawkins 1988; Croft 1990), although the precise formulation is not identical). First, the constraints may be *absolute*[3] or *statistical*. In other words, they can differ in the degree to which we may expect exceptions. This might immediately seem problematic, since how can we state a constraint on possible human languages that may be violated? However, it is important to realize

---

[3] The term *absolute universal* is sometimes used, by others, for substantive or formal universals that simply constrain languages so that they all have a certain property.

that a statistically significant skewing of the distribution of languages is as worthy of explanation as an absolute one.[4]

Secondly, the format of the constraint can typically be characterized as *parametric* or *hierarchical*. This difference is related to the logical relationships between typological dimensions:

Parametric universals. These describe a co-occurrence relation between different types, so that when one type occurs, so does the other and vice versa. They are expressed logically as:

$$\forall L[(P_1(L) \leftrightarrow P_2(L))\&(P_2(L) \leftrightarrow P_3(L))\& \cdots \&(P_{n-1}(L) \leftrightarrow P_n(L))]$$

where P_i is some property of a language L[5] that differentiates between a type T_i and T_i', where a prime here indicates an opposite type.[6] This logical statement can be paraphrased in prose as something like: 'for all languages, if a language has property 1, then it will have property 2, and vice versa. Furthermore, if a language has property 2, then it will have property 3, and vice versa. In fact, a language either has all the properties from 1 to n, or none of them.'

Hierarchical universals. These also describe co-occurrence relations, but crucially they are asymmetric across types. The logical expression is as:

$$\forall L[(P_1(L) \rightarrow P_2(L))\&(P_2(L) \rightarrow P_3(L))\& \cdots \&(P_{n-1}(L) \rightarrow P_n(L))]$$

Again, this logical statement can be paraphrased in prose as: 'for all languages, if a language has property 1, then it will have property 2, but not necessarily vice versa. Furthermore, if that language has property 2, then it will have property 3. In fact, a language which has some numbered property will have all the properties from that number up to n.'

---

[4] This leads to the problem of identifying statistical significance (as will be discussed in Chapter 2), but this problem is equally present for absolute universals. For example, imagine a typology categorizes languages into three types: A, B, and C. Let us say in a typologist's sample that 99% of languages are type A, 1% are type B, and none is type C. From an absolute stance, we would conclude that human languages can be A or B but never C. However, what if type C was simply missing from the sample but observable elsewhere? If this were the case, then A, B, and C should be given the same status in absolute terms. A statistical approach, on the other hand, would enable us to say that A was significantly more common than B or C.

[5] For convenience we can simply abstract away from L in the expression of these universals in other places in this book.

[6] This formulation relies on a binary typology. However, other typologies can be easily reduced to this case.

The simplest hierarchical universal involving two type dimensions is traditionally termed an *implicational universal*. These may also be written using the symbol $\supset$ instead of $\rightarrow$.

The last two diagrams in Figure 1.1(*e* and *f*) are examples of parametric and hierarchical universals respectively. The first universal parametrically relates verb/object order and adposition/noun-phrase order. This can be written as $VO \leftrightarrow Prep$, where $VO' \equiv OV$ and $Prep' \equiv Postp$. A prose paraphrase of this universal would be something like: 'All VO languages are Prep languages, and vice versa.' The second universal is different in that it rules out only one of the four logically possible types, $VO\&SComp$. This universal can be written, $VO \rightarrow CompS$, where $CompS' \equiv SComp$. This can be paraphrased: 'All VO languages are CompS languages.'

These two universals are examples of the simplest kinds of parametric and hierarchical universals, relating only two binary types. The first constrains languages to 2 out of 4 possible types, and the second to 3 out of 4 possible types. In general, parametric universals constrain attested languages to 2 out of 2^n possibilities, and hierarchical universals constrain to $n + 1$ out of 2^n. So, even for a small number of types, these universals are highly predictive.

Hierarchies

The second type of universal is of special interest to linguists as it defines an asymmetrical hierarchy of types. These are often written using the $>$ operator to express relative height on the hierarchy. A universal such as:

$$(A \rightarrow B)\&(B \rightarrow C)$$

would be written:

$$C > B > A$$

Languages can be defined by their position on such a hierarchy, since any language with a property corresponding to a type low on the hierarchy will also have the properties of the types higher on the hierarchy. The Greenberg (1963: 78) universal, 'languages with dominant VSO [verb–subject–object] order are always prepositional', can be expressed as $VSO \rightarrow Prep$. We could also rewrite this as a hierarchy $Prep > VSO$, and English could be placed halfway up this hierarchy as having *Prep* but not *VSO*. This is not usually done for such simple implicational universals, however. Instead, the hierarchy is reserved for 'chained implications' or multi-typed hierarchical universals in our terms.

Table 1.1. *Grammatical number on nouns*

Plural	Dual	Trial/paucal
−	−	−
+	−	−
+	+	−
+	+	+

A well-known example of a hierarchy is given by Croft (1990: 96–8),[7] referring to the possible expression of grammatical number on nouns:

plural > dual > trial/paucal

This corresponds to the universal:

(trial/paucal → dual)&(dual → plural)

In other words, if a language marks trial or paucal number on nouns, it will also mark dual; if it marks dual, it will mark plural. This hierarchy constrains human languages to four out of eight possibilities (adapted from Croft 1990: 97):

1. languages with only one noun form (languages without a category of number);
2. languages with singular and plural forms for nouns;[8]
3. languages with singular, dual, and plural forms for nouns;
4. languages with singular, dual, plural, and trial/paucal forms for nouns.

Another common way of visualizing this hierarchical universal is as a table where each row is a possible human language and + means that a language is of a particular type (see Table 1.1).

---

[7] Note that Croft uses the < operator where we will be using >. Croft's use of this operator reflects relative *markedness*, a typological property to which we will return briefly in the next chapter.

[8] Notice that, as it is presented here, the hierarchy makes no mention of singular number. It makes sense to talk of nouns having a number form only if there is something to contrast it with. So, it would be meaningless to say that a language had a plural form for nouns and no other form. The singular form is not mentioned in the hierarchy and can be assumed to be the default with which the others are contrasted. Alternatively we could add the 'singular' at the top of the hierarchy (as Croft does). Strictly speaking this would add an extra type of language to the predicted set: one that had no number at all (not even singular). However, this type cannot be distinguished from one that has only singular.

Table 1.2. *The contrapositive number hierarchy*

Plural'	Dual'	Trial/paucal'
−	−	−
−	−	+
−	+	+
+	+	+

Although not required by the logical structure of a universal, a typically unspoken requirement of a hierarchy such as this is that there is an example language for each position on the hierarchy. English, for example, would be positioned on the second row.

Each implicational statement has a logical equivalent related to it by *modus tollens*. The implication $P \rightarrow Q$ is identical, truth conditionally, to $\neg Q \rightarrow \neg P$. In terms of binary types, this means that if $A \rightarrow B$ is a universal, then so is $B' \rightarrow A'$. I will refer to this as the *contrapositive universal*. The hierarchy above thus has a contrapositive equivalent:

$$\text{trial}'/\text{paucal}' > \text{dual}' > \text{plural}'$$

where the prime symbol on these types simply refers to a language which *does not* mark that number category on any nouns. In other words, if a language does not have plural number, then it will not have dual number; if a language does not have dual number, it will not have trial or paucal number. In Chapter 3, the choice between a hierarchy and its contrapositive 'twin' will be shown to reflect on its explanation. The contrapositive table of possible languages (Table 1.2) is simply a mirror image of Table 1.1 (here, English would be on the third row):

The evidence of fit

I have said that language universals show the 'appearance of design' in that there is a fit of form to function. The search for this fit underlies an approach to the explanation of universals that is usually referred to as the *functional approach*. This term appears to be used mainly to set up an opposition between linguists interested in language function and those following the *generative* or *formal* approach (to which we will turn shortly).

Perhaps the most extensive and critical review of the structure of functional explanation currently available is Newmeyer (1998), who has this to say about the variety of explanations and the problems of defining what *functionalism* actually means:

Those who share the functionalist orientation differ in their basic assumptions far more than do those who are committed to the generativist approach. This is partly a consequence of there being a lot more possible ways that one can be against some theoretical conception (the compartmentalization of form) than one can be for it. Saying that the formal properties of language are not characterized as a system unto themselves leaves open a myriad of possibilities as to how they *should be* characterized.   (§5)

I . . . characterize as 'functionalism' any approach that emdodies the following three positions. . . . First, the links between formal properties of grammar and their semantic and pragmatic functions are tight enough to preclude any significant methodological or analytical 'parcelling out' of form. Second, to a significant degree, the formal properties of grammar are motivated by the functions that language carries out, in particular its function of conveying meaning in communication. And third, by means of integrating functional explanation with typological investigation, one can explain why certain grammatical features in the languages of the world are more common than others and why, for particular languages, the appearance of one feature often implies the appearance of another.   (§5.4)

Newmeyer's definition of the functional approach is consistent with the characterization used in this book, where functionalism is seen as being concerned with explaining the structure of language (in particular language universals) by finding evidence of fit between that structure and language use.

Types of functional explanation

Various authors, in reviewing explanations for language universals, have pointed out the different aspects of language use that have been called upon in functional explanation (see e.g. Comrie 1981: 26–9; Hawkins 1988: 8–18; Hurford 1990: 94–6; Croft 1990: 252–6; Hall 1992: 27–32; and references therein). In this section we will look at some well-known examples that appeal to four rather different perspectives on use.

First, Comrie (1981: 28) notes that 'the existence of first or second person reflexive forms in a language implies the existence of third person reflexive forms'. He appeals to *pragmatics* to explain this constraint. Within the same English utterance, different instances of *I* or *me* always refer to the same entity. Similarly, almost all instances of *we* or *you* will refer to the same thing (unless the speaker points at different people during the utterance). On the other hand, third person pronouns are regularly non-coreferential in an utterance. Comrie suggests that the reflexive/non-reflexive distinction is therefore more important functionally for making co-referentiality unambiguous in third person referents than first or second person referents.

Another type of explanation appeals to *iconicity*, or the isomorphism of sign and signified. One of Greenberg's (1963: 93) universals states 'if both the derivation and inflection follow the root, or they both precede the root, the derivation is always between the root and the inflection'. For example, in the English word *computations*, the derivational affix *-ation* comes before the inflectional affix *-s*. Bybee's (1985) explanation for this is that the formal closeness of an affix to its stem iconically reflects its conceptual closeness—the degree to which the semantics of the affix affects solely the meaning of the word. In Croft's (1990: 176) words, 'derivational morphology alters the lexical meaning of the root, sometimes drastically, whereas inflectional morphology only adds semantic properties or embeds the concept denoted by the root into the larger linguistic context'.

A third type of explanation appeals to the structure of *discourse*. An interesting and complex example is DuBois's (1987) explanation of the tendency for languages' case systems to pattern as *nominative–accusative* or as *ergative*. Briefly, the nominative–accusative pattern, which reserves special marking for the object of a transitive as opposed to the subject of transitives and intransitives, represents an iconic patterning of agents versus non-agents in language. The ergative system, on the other hand, matches a preferred argument structure in discourse. DuBois argues, using text counts, that most clauses in discourse involve only one or zero nominal arguments. This is because transitive subjects are usually 'given' topics and therefore pronominal. This means that full noun phrases are most often subjects of intransitives or objects of transitives, hence the special marking reserved for subjects of transitives in ergative case systems. DuBois goes on to extend his analysis to split-ergative patterns, but a full treatment of his approach would be beyond the purposes of this review.

Finally, *processing* has often been appealed to in the explanation of universals. Cutler *et al.* (1985) aim to explain the cross-linguistic preference for suffixes, as opposed to prefixes, in terms of the way in which language is processed by hearers in real time. The crucial feature of this processing is that it is constrained by the left-to-right, serial nature of speech. The start of a word is clearly received by the processor before the end, and the assumption is that work starts on processing input as soon as it arrives. Simplifying the situation somewhat, Cutler *et al.* point out that early lexical access is preferred by hearers, so the placing of salient information early in the word aids processing. If lexical access is stem-based—as they argue from experimental evidence—then the tendency for languages to be suffixal matches the preference of the processor.

Aspects of function

The brief review above highlights the main feature functional explanations have in common: universals are 'explained' by demonstrating that their content matches some feature of language use. Typically, some difference between pairs of linguistic objects matches a similar difference in the use of those objects (where *objects* is taken to mean anything that corresponds to a *type*). So, differences between reflexives of second and third person correspond to differences in the use of those reflexives in utterances. Differences in the position of derivational and inflectional affixes correspond to differences in the use of those affixes to signal changes in meaning. The differential marking of transitive subjects in ergative languages corresponds to their special role in discourse. The cross-linguistic difference in the distribution of suffixes and prefixes mirrors the left-to-right processing of words. In this way, all these explanations appeal to the fit of universals to function.

However, we have so far been rather vague about what constitutes 'function'. The explanations above rely on features of language use, but these features are all very different. For example, Hyman (1984) makes a distinction between two types of function:

Unfortunately, there is disagreement on the meaning of 'functional' as applied in this context. While everyone would agree that explanations in terms of communication and the nature of discourse are functional ... explanations in terms of cognition, the nature of the brain, etc., are considered functional by some but not other linguists. The distinction appears to be that cognitive or psycholinguistic explanations involve formal operations that the human mind can vs. cannot accommodate or 'likes' vs. 'does not like', etc., while pragmatic or sociolinguistic explanations involve (formal?) operations that a human society or individual within a society can vs. cannot accommodate or likes vs. does not like.   (Hyman 1984: 67–8, cited in Hurford 1990)

This distinction can be rephrased as a difference between characteristics of the *users of language* and characteristics of *the purpose of language use*. Hurford (1990: 96) makes a useful analogy with the design of a spade. Parts of the spade are clearly designed with the *purpose* of the spade in mind, the sharp metal blade, for example. Other parts of the spade appear to be designed more for the *user*, such as its hand-sized handle and the length of its shaft. We can see that both aspects of the use of the spade have influenced its design—the spade's structure fits its function because of this.

It has been suggested (e.g. Hall 1992: 32) that the functional approach suffers from a lack of cohesion. This stems partly from the fact that the study of the purpose-based aspects of function and the user-based aspects of function belong to rather different research traditions in linguistics. In principle, however, I believe that this need not be the case. The distinction highlighted by Hyman and Hurford can be subsumed by a view that looks solely at the *process* of language use. All aspects of the spade's design can be explained by carefully examining the aspects of the digging process—the user of the spade and the purpose of the spade are unified in this act.

The various aspects of function utilized in the explanations of the last section might be similarly viewed as aspects of language processing. Givón (1985: 189) argues that iconic tendencies in language result from the relative ease of processing forms which are 'isomorphic to experience'. The work of Sperber and Wilson (1986) in Relevance Theory also places a great deal of importance on processing effort in explaining pragmatic effects. The discourse features that DuBois (1987) appeals to must similarly have their ultimate explanation in terms of processing. For example, the reason that given entities are pronominalized is presumably related to the relative effort it takes for a hearer to recover the referent for a given versus a new entity.

Although it looks as if there are a multitude of different ways in which language use can impact on universals, many of these can ultimately be reduced to pressures of processing language in real time. Processing here is a general term for *both* the act of parsing (i.e. mapping an acoustic wave onto a corresponding message and interpretation) and production (i.e. the mapping from communicative intention to articulation). A functional explanation for a language universal therefore is a statement of fit between that universal and the pressures of processing. For the functionalist, a universal is explained if it appears to be designed to ease processing. I do not claim to have shown that all functional explanations can be reduced to considerations of language processing, merely that this is probably the case for most. The rest of this book will therefore deal with explanations that appeal to pressures on production and perception of language, and I believe that the approach will be relevant to all functional explanations. Another reason to concentrate on this aspect of language use is that there are available *a priori* theories of language processing that have been compared with cross-linguistic evidence. This serves to deflect a common criticism of functional explanations (e.g. Lass 1980)—that they are constructed 'after the event' in the sense that there tends to be an *ad hoc* search for functions that match the universals to be explained.

UG and universals

As mentioned earlier, the functional approach to explaining language universals contrasts with the other major paradigm in modern linguistics. As Hall (1992: 2) puts it, 'much, perhaps most, recent work within the functional approach either explicitly or implicitly uses the Chomskyan paradigm as a point of departure or a point of contrast'.[9] One of the purposes of this book, particularly Chapter 5, is to show that this opposition is spurious at best, and rather damaging for the explanatory adequacy of both approaches.

This apparently opposing paradigm goes under a number of different names—*Chomskyan, generative, formal,* and *innatist* (or *nativist*)—all of them somewhat misleading. First, just as with the functionalist approach, these terms suggest an unwarranted degree of coherence. There are currently several broad theoretical programmes to which these labels could be applied. For example, *Principles and Parameters* (or *Government and Binding Theory*) (Chomsky 1981), the *Minimalist Program* (Marantz 1995), and *Optimality Theory* (e.g. Grimshaw 1997). All of these are Chomskyan in the sense of directly expanding on the basic suggestions of Chomsky's own work, but there is a great deal of diversity even here. None of the theories within these programs is strictly generative or formal (although formalization is possible), but the name seems to have stuck from the early days of transformational grammar. There *are* formal theories of syntax around, however; *HPSG* (Pollard and Sag 1994) is the most popular at the moment. On the other hand, these theories could not really be called 'Chomskyan'.

Syntactic theory and universals

The final term in our list—innatist—is perhaps the most useful for our purposes. It refers to an underlying idea that, in achieving explanatory adequacy, a theory of syntax must be telling us something about the human brain. In particular, it tells us about properties of the brain that are biologically given as opposed to given by the environment. Syntactic theory, in the innatist sense, is a theory of the knowledge of language with which we are born. This is important, because any innate component to our knowledge of language can be assumed to be shared by every member of our species.[10] If this is so, then we have a ready-made explanation for universal properties of languages (Hoekstra and Kooij 1988).

It seems then that the innatist and functionalist approaches are inevitably in competition as explanations of language universals. It is important to realize, however, that the central question that each approach is attempting to answer is different. Simplifying the situation drastically,

---

[9] The syntactic (as opposed to phonological) bias of this book should be clear by this stage. The following review ignores the corresponding tension between functional and generative approaches to phonology.

[10] This is not *necessarily* the case, of course. It is possible that some degree of variation in innate knowledge of language may be uncovered.

the difference can be characterized in terms of questions posed to, and answers given by, an imaginary functionalist, and an imaginary formalist:

The innatist approach

Central question: 'How are languages acquired from the degenerate data available to the child?'

Answer: 'A richly specified innate language acquisition device (LAD) in combination with the primary linguistic data (PLD) is sufficient for the task.'

Subsidiary question: 'Why are there constraints on cross-linguistic variation?'

Answer: 'The structure of the LAD constrains variation.'

The functional–typological approach

Central question: 'Why do the constraints on variation have a particular form?'

Answer: 'The particular observed constraints are the reflex of language use.'

Subsidiary question: 'How are languages acquired?'

Answer: 'The data available to the child are rich enough for language to be acquired using general-purpose learning mechanisms.'

The richly structured, innate UG or LAD posited by generative syntax is not proposed in response to the hierarchical and parametric universals uncovered by typological research. Instead, the prime concern is the problem of language acquisition in the absence of necessary experience—a variant of *Plato's problem* in Chomsky's (1986) terms. A brief review of the solution given by the principles and parameters approach will make this clearer (for a more in-depth review, see e.g. Haegeman 1991: 10–20).[11]

Principles and parameters

Levels of adequacy

An interesting feature of the Chomskyan approach to linguistic theory is the recognition of two levels of adequacy of a theory. First, a theory is *descriptively adequate* if it goes beyond a description of the linguistic data

---

[11] Recent developments in syntactic theory suggest a trend away from parametric theories of acquisition and variation. Instead, variation is being devolved to individual lexical entries. The idea of a core of invariant principles which constrain variation is still a central one, however.

and accounts for a native speaker's intuitions about the grammaticality of utterances. In order that it can do this it must take into account that language has two very different aspects: its external aspect and its internal aspect. External language (or E-language) is that aspect of language that is directly observable as writing or speech. Internal language (or I-language), on the other hand, is the specific knowledge of a person that allows her to produce or comprehend a particular language. I-language is, therefore, the domain of enquiry for a descriptively adequate theory of syntax in the Chomskyan approach.

The preferred, though not sole, method of studying I-language is through careful elicitation of judgements of grammaticality. These judgements are assumed to abstract away from factors that influence E-language such as processing constraints. This assumption underlies the *autonomy thesis*: the idea that I-language makes no reference to system-external factors (e.g. Chomsky 1975, cited in Newmeyer 1992: 783). This is perhaps another reason for the apparent opposition of formal and functional approaches. We will return to this issue in Chapter 5.

The second level of adequacy of a theory of syntax—*explanatory adequacy*—is achieved if it can account for speakers' acquisition of the knowledge embodied in I-language. As noted above, the Chomskyan approach relies on the degeneracy of input data, the argument being that the acquisition of language can be achieved only given innate syntactic knowledge. Clearly, not all language can be innately coded, otherwise there would be no cross-linguistic variation. In principles and parameters theory, this variation is assumed to result from the setting of various parameters in response to the environment during acquisition. These parameter settings interact with an inventory of invariant principles which (in combination with a set of lexical items) make up the mature I-language of a speaker.

The contents of UG

UG, therefore, has two properties (from Haegeman 1991: 14):

1. 'UG contains a set of absolute universals, notions and principles which do not vary from one language to the next.'

2. 'There are language-specific properties which are not fully determined by UG but which vary cross-linguistically. For these properties a range of choices [parameters] is offered by UG.'

The problem of language acquisition now boils down to the setting of parameters given appropriate triggering experience extracted from the PLD. Compared to the task of learning a language using some kind of general-purpose learning mechanism, this parameter setting is relatively trivial. In this way, the principles and parameters approach appears to solve

Plato's problem for language. Notice, however, that the very existence of this problem is not universally accepted:

How good is this argument? On the one hand, it seems to me highly plausible that there are *some* innately represented features of human language in the human species, and that these do facilitate language acquisition. On the other hand, there is a major issue that has not received the attention and critical scrutiny it deserves within the Chomskyan literature, namely: what exactly *can* the child infer from positive evidence? what kinds of learning strategies *do* children actually adopt, both in language and in other cognitive domains? and *are* these strategies systematically incapable of explaining language acquisition without the innateness hypothesis?
(Hawkins 1988: 7)

We should treat with some caution claims that features of language are unlearnable without the particular type of innate knowledge embodied in the principles and parameters approach. However, it is clear that, at the very least, any kind of domain specific knowledge will aid the acquisition process.

Constraints on variation

Putting the learnability issue aside, what types of constraints on variation can this theory explain? First, the principles of grammar can directly constrain languages to be all of a certain type. For example, the universal that languages allow sentences to have subjects is trivially predicted from the extended projection principle, which includes a requirement that clauses have a position for a subject.

Secondly, parametric universals also seem to be easily explained in this approach. The setting of a parameter to one 'position' or another in the process of acquisition has typically many effects on the ultimate grammatical structure of the language. If this switching of settings in acquisition is the only (non-lexical) way in which languages can vary, and all other things are equal, then properties associated with a particular parameter setting should give rise to a parametric universal. So, for example, one parameter discussed by Haegeman (1991: 450–1) determines the overtness of *wh*-movement in a language. English has overt *wh*-movement (that is, expressions like *which, who,* and so on visibly move to the front of a clause), whereas Chinese has non-overt *wh*-movement (the equivalent expressions in this language appear *in situ,* but are assumed to move at some level in order that they can be interpreted correctly). The differences in the sentence structures of these two languages that this parameter difference creates could form the basis of a set of binary types which would then be related by a parametric universal.

Although it might seem counter-intuitive given the nature of parameters, hierarchical universals can also be expressed in this theory. A multi-valued parameter (or a set of binary parameters) can, in principle, 'point to' the position of a language on an implicational hierarchy. The possible *governing categories* in a language provide us with an example. These determine constraints on the positions of anaphors and their antecedents and appear to form a hierarchically ordered set. Manzini and Wexler (1987) propose a five-valued parameter which inputs into a definition of a governing category:

> **Governing category.** γ is a governing category for α if: γ is the minimal category that contains α and a governor for α and has either
> 1. a subject, or
> 2. an Infl, or
> 3. a tense, or
> 4. a 'referential' tense, or
> 5. a 'root' tense
>
> depending on the value of the parameter.

Now, the details of this definition and exactly how it affects the distribution of anaphors need not concern us here. The interesting feature of this definition is that different settings of the parameter give rise to different degrees to which anaphors may be separated from their antecedents. In fact, according to Manzini and Wexler (1987), the grammatical domains within which anaphors and their antecedents can both occur form subset relations down the list of parameter settings above. In this way, hierarchical patterns of variation are expressible in principles and parameters theory.

A careful study of the typological correlates of parameters such as these is conspicuously absent from the literature and probably will remain that way. This is partly due to the gradual rejection of parametric variation in favour of lexical variation, and partly due to the nature of formal syntactic research, favouring as it does the in-depth analysis of a few languages rather than the shallow analysis of many. Another reason why parameters do not readily translate as universals, however, is that their effects are highly interactive. The grammar of a language, and hence its resultant typological type(s), is a result of all the principles and parameter settings working together to constrain the set of grammatical sentences. If a particular observed universal is to be explained syntactically, it is likely to involve not one parameter but an examination of the possibilities allowed by the totality of UG.

Finally, whilst it is in principle possible that all the different logical forms of constraint described in this chapter can be expressed by a combination of parameters and principles, it is hard to see how this paradigm could be used to explain statistical as opposed to absolute universals. Of course, this is not its job (as pointed out in the previous section), but *at the very least* it leaves some scope for other forms of explanation.

The problem of linkage

The previous two sections have outlined quite different approaches to the problem of explaining language universals. I have suggested that both approaches eventually have their place in a complete view of universals. Although the full justification for this point of view must wait for later chapters, a basic flaw in each approach on its own should be pointed out here.

First, although the innatist line of reasoning has many virtues—for example, it is explicit about the mechanism through which universals emerge—it fails to tackle the puzzle of fit. For example, the order of derivational and inflectional affixes could conceivably be constrained by some model of generative morphology. This constraint would then be assumed to be part of the biological endowment of the language learner, and would serve partially to alleviate the problem of learning language. As a side effect, Greenberg's (1963) universal mentioned earlier would be explained. The problem with this is that it misses the fact that this universal *appears to be designed* with iconicity in mind. Our imaginary (extreme) nativist would have to assume that it was simply coincidence that the formal constraint happened to be iconic to 'conceptual closeness' (Bybee 1985). So, perhaps this *is* a coincidence, or the theory of iconicity is sufficiently *ad hoc* in its formulation to be ignored. If, on the other hand, this fit of universal to processing can be demonstrated over and over again, this appears to undermine the innatist autonomy assumption (though, see Chapter 5 for a different perspective).

The biggest flaw in the functional approach has already been mentioned. It highlights the fact that universals fit pressures imposed by language use, but this on its own does not constitute an explanation of anything. The innatist approach links universals to acquisition, so that constraints on cross-linguistic variation are the *direct consequence* of constraints on the acquisition (and mental representation) of language. The functionalist approach fails to make this link between *explanans* and *explanandum*, leaving the real puzzle, the puzzle of fit, unexplained. Bybee (1988: 352) refers to this as the 'how question'—given a set of generalizations about language she asks, 'how do such generalizations arise in language? What are the *mechanisms* that bring such a state of affairs about?' Hall (1988: 323) argues that a proposed explanation must 'attempt to establish the mechanism by which underlying pressure or pressures actually instantiate in language the structural pattern under investigation'. The feeling that there is something missing from functional explanations is also echoed by

Croft's (1993: 21–2) complaint that linguistic theories of adaptation (i.e. fit) do not match up to biological ones:

the sorts of explanations made by typologists are essentially adaptive ones: language structures are the way they are because of their adaptation to the function(s) of language . . . In this respect linguistics also parallels biology.

However, the philosophical analogy between linguistic functional explanations and biological adaptation is not always fully worked out in linguistics.

To be completely explicit, we can formulate the following problem:

The problem of linkage. Given a set of observed constraints on cross-linguistic variation, and a corresponding pattern of functional preference, an explanation of this fit will solve the problem: how does the latter give rise to the former?

This book is an attempt to answer this question in a very general way (essentially to fill the gap in Figure 1.2), but with examples from specific universals and specific theories of processing. As such, the main aim is not to uncover new constraints on variation, nor to find new functional asymmetries, although modelling the link between these two inevitably leads us to some new predictions both about universals and about processing.

In order to test that the proposed solution to the problem of linkage leads to the correct conclusions, I have adopted a simulation methodology. The theoretical assumptions of this book are therefore formalized as computer programs and tested against the available cross-linguistic evidence. This approach is fairly unusual in the linguistic literature, but it does have some precedents—for example, the evolutionary simulations of Hurford (1989) and other papers, Jules Levin's dialectology simulations reported by Keller (1994: 100), and Bakker's (1994) computational work on typological theory testing in the Functional Grammar framework. The adoption of this methodology allows us to keep the general answer to the problem above separate from the specific examples of the explanatory approach (e.g. the accessibility hierarchy and Hawkins's (1994*b*) performance theory). The

Figure 1.2. The problem of linkage. Compare this with the solution, Figure 5.3.

former is encoded as a simulation platform, and the latter as the particular initial conditions of a simulation run.

Overview

The rest of the book divides roughly into two parts. The first half goes into a theoretical approach to the problem of linkage and shows how this approach can be modelled computationally in order to test its validity with respect to particular explanations in the literature. The latter half of the book then reflects on the implications of the proposed approach for typology, functional explanation, and particularly innate theories of language variation.

The following chapter builds up a picture of the link between universals and function by considering in some detail Hawkins's (1994*b*) recent performance theory of word-order universals. For this explanation to be complete, it is argued that the parser must be acting as a *selection mechanism* within the cycle of language acquisition and use. This view is shown to be related to characterizations of language change as an *invisible hand process* and to more general models of complex adaptive systems. Given this, a computational model of this system is built and tested using Hawkins's performance metric. It is shown that this model gives us a mechanism by which universals emerge, and as a bonus derives the prototypical time course of language change. The chapter ends with some discussion about the relationship of universals and *markedness* given this model.

Although the simulation seems to be successful at this stage, the types of universal on which it is tested are quite simple (e.g. two-valued parametric). Chapter 3 aims to extend the approach to explain the paradigm multi-valued implicational universal: the accessibility hierarchy (AH). To do this, certain changes need to be made to the model to allow for multiple stable types to coexist. Once again, Hawkins's (1994*b*) performance theory is applied to the task, but the initial results are disappointing. It is argued instead that Hawkins's explanation needs to be extended to a *competing motivations* approach in which speaker and hearer are in conflict in the acquisition/use cycle. Two types of complexity are proposed which both input into the simulation; if these shift in relative prominence over time, the end result is a dynamic situation with the correct hierarchical pattern of linguistic variation moving geographically over time. This important result is explained using a simple graphical formalism based on graph theory, and predictions are made and tested regarding more subtle distinctions in the strategies of relativization available to speakers. Finally suggestions are made for the extension of this approach to other hierarchical universals.

Having made the case for a selection-based solution to the problem of linkage, the focus changes in Chapter 4 to the implications for the modes of explanation reviewed above. A failure in the functional approach is highlighted when other processing pressures on the comprehension of relative clauses are compared with the cross-linguistic evidence. Specifically a review of the psycholinguistic literature suggests that there is an asymmetrical processing preference for *parallel function* relatives. This appears not to be reflected in any language. There seems, therefore, to be something constraining the process of linguistic adaptation. It is argued that the best candidate for such a (meta-)constraint is an innate language faculty in the Chomskyan sense. This conclusion is strengthened by a careful examination of a case where parallel function apparently *is* expressed in a language. If the innate LAD can constrain the emergence of relative-clause universals, it is probable that there will be other mismatches between form and function that can be similarly understood. The chapter ends with a look at animacy, length, heavy NP shift, and the English genitive in the light of this.

Chapter 5 takes the link between function and innateness one stage further with a review of the most recent literature on the biological evolution of the human language faculty. The very autonomous features of the LAD that appear to put its study in direct opposition to the functional enterprise are argued to have a type of functional explanation themselves. This means that the solution to the problem of linkage (the missing piece in Figure 1.2) that was proposed in the first half of this book needs to be elaborated to take into account other forms of adaptation. A comparison of five different authors' views on the origin of the subjacency condition serves to highlight the lack of consensus in the literature on this subject.

Finally, in this necessarily speculative chapter and in the conclusion, Chapter 6, some suggestions are made about the directions future research might take, especially in the light of the approach taken in this book.

2 The Impact of Processing on Word Order

In order to explore how pressures on language use can explain language universals, some theory of use must be put forward.[1] This chapter examines such a theory—the performance theory of John Hawkins (e.g. Hawkins 1994a)—that has been mainly used to explain word-order universals. Hawkins's theory provides us with an explicit quantification of the relative parsing complexity of various orders of constituents. The main thrust of this chapter will be to solve the problem of linkage in this specific case: how does a difference in parsing complexity lead to a difference in cross-linguistic distribution? Although this is a quite specific example of the fit of universals to processing, the solution will be developed in general terms and extended to other examples later in the book.

Hawkins's processing theory and word order

Hawkins's performance theory (Hawkins 1990, 1992a,b, 1993, 1994a) has been applied to two separate but related explanatory domains. First, he examines the choice of word orders in performance. This relates to rearrangement rules such as English heavy NP shift, and also to the choice of orderings in 'free-order' constructions. Secondly, and more importantly for us, Hawkins looks in detail at the distribution of basic word orders, grammaticalized in competence grammars across languages. It is this second domain—that of word-order universals—that is the central concern of this chapter.

Perhaps the most important set of word-order universals that Hawkins tackles relates to *head ordering*. That is, the *statistical* tendency for languages to have a consistent positioning of heads (the syntactically central elements of constituents) relative to non-heads across the phrasal categories in the competence grammar.

In these Japanese examples (from Shibatani 1990: 257), the heads all follow the non-heads (in other words, Japanese can be characterized as a

---

[1] Some sections of this chapter have been published as Kirby (1994).

head-final language):

(2.1) Taroo ga   Hanako ni   hon   o   yatta
      Taro   NOM Hanako DAT book ACC gave
      'Taro gave a book to Hanako'

(2.2) sono san-nin   no ookina otoko
      that three-person of big   man
      'those three big men'

(2.3) Taroo no hon
      Taro of book
      'Taro's book'

In Example 2.1, nominal relations are expressed as particles that follow the nouns, and the verb follows the object. In Example 2.2, the head noun follows the demonstrative, numeral, and adjective, and, in Example 2.3, the head noun follows the genitive.

Hawkins uses a large sample of languages classified into types (Hawkins 1983) to demonstrate the validity of these empirical generalizations, expressing distributional universals as ratios of exemplifying languages to non-exemplifying languages (e.g. there is a clear tendency for SOV languages to be postpositional—93 per cent in Hawkins's sample). Matthew Dryer's work on word-order universals (e.g. Dryer 1991, 1992) goes further than Hawkins's, since it takes into account the idea that simple language counts cannot be used to demonstrate *statistically significant* differences in numbers of languages, because statistical tests require items in a sample to be independent of each other. In order to meet the criteria of independence a language sample would need to consist of languages that were genetically and areally unrelated to each other. Consequently, any such sample would probably be too small to make any significant generalizations. I will return to Dryer's work later, but for now I would suggest simply that correlations as strong as SOV&Po, above, in a large sample are presumably significant without consideration of genetic/areal groupings.

Of course, both of these samples rely on being able to identify the basic word-order types of languages. Comrie (1981: 82) has this to say about some of the problems that are involved:

Although . . . there is general agreement as to the basic word order, there are many languages where the situation is less clear-cut . . . When we classify English as being basically SVO, we abstract away from the fact that in special questions the word order of the *wh-* element is determined not by its grammatical relation, but rather by a general rule that places such elements sentence initially, thus giving rise to such OSV orders as *who(m) did John see?* Even in many languages that are often described as having free word order, there is some good indication that one of the orders is more basic than the others. In Russian, for instance, any permutation of S, O, and V will give a grammatical sentence, but the order SVO is much more frequent than all the other orders put together . . .

The parser

Hawkins's main parsing principle, early immediate constituent recognition (or EIC), is expressed as a preference of the parser for as much constituency information as possible in the shortest time. Hawkins argues for this preference with reference to the literature on parsing and also defines a method for quantifying this preference. This section summarizes Hawkins's arguments, which are treated more fully in Hawkins (1990).

Modules of mind

In the dedication of *The Modularity of Mind* (Fodor 1983), Fodor quotes a comment made by Merrill Garrett that parsing is basically 'a reflex'. He argues that various modules of the mind dealing with input—including the parser[2]—have reflex-like properties. Some of these properties are:

Domain specificity. Analysis of highly eccentric stimuli (such as acoustic waves organized into sentences) requires a set of information that is specific to the domain of those stimuli.

Mandatoriness. The response of an input system to a stimulus provided by sensory transducers is obligatory—it is impossible not to attempt to parse a sentence, for example, if you hear it.

Encapsulation. Input systems have only very limited access to high-level information in the form of expectations or beliefs. So, for example, it should be possible to parse a sentence without *necessarily* bringing higher-level knowledge into play in the parsing of that sentence.

Speed. Input systems are surprisingly fast. This speed of operation is linked closely with mandatoriness: if an input system acts like a reflex, then computation can—indeed, must—begin immediately the stimulus is presented. Time is not wasted 'making up our minds' about how to deal with the input, as Fodor puts it.

---

[2] Though I am treating the parser as one of Fodor's 'input systems' it is possible that similar principles may play a part in the generation of output. The parser, therefore, can be seen as *one* of the processing mechanisms mediating between the two parts of the Saussurean sign. It may turn out that processing considerations have a large part to play in the choice of orderings of sentences produced, but for the moment I will be looking only at the role they have in comprehension (see later).

Hawkins uses these features of modules of mind—particularly manda-toriness and speed—to argue that the parser will construct hierarchical structure as rapidly as possible when given enough information to do so. The suggestion that modules are domain specific and encapsulated should lead us to prefer a model of processing that relies only on information specific to the parser—that is, a grammar; and feedback from other parts of the language system, such as pragmatic knowledge, should not be pos-tulated. Frazier and Rayner (1988) give empirical support to this claim by comparing reading times of sentences with sentential subjects with those where the subject is extraposed (e.g. *That both of the conjoined twins sur-vived the operation is remarkable* versus *It is remarkable that both of the conjoined twins survived the operation*). The difference in reading times between the pairs of sentences was similar whether they were presented in or out of a context that introduced the relevant referents. This suggests that non-syntactic information is not used to alleviate processing difficulty.

Deterministic parsing

Another important feature of the human parser is determinism. The sys-tem modelling the human parser described by Marcus (1980: §1.1) cru-cially relies on this feature:

> **The determinism hypothesis.**   The syntax of any natural language can be parsed by a machine which operates 'strictly deterministically' in that it does not simulate a non-deterministic machine.

In Hawkins's model of the parser, then, a mother node is built above a syntactic category immediately and obligatorily, as soon as its presence is guaranteed by the input and the phrase structure rules of the language. In general, this will occur whenever a syntactic category *uniquely determines* a mother node. These mother node constructing categories (MNCCs) are similar to heads in traditional syntactic theory, but may also include some closed-class function words such as determiners which uniquely construct noun phrases. So, for example, in the verb phrase *tended the garden*, *tended* can construct the VP, and *the* and *garden* can both construct the NP (see Figure 2.1). This gives us Hawkins's first parsing mechanism:

> **Mother node construction.**   During parsing, if an MNCC is discov-ered, then the determined mother node is built above the constructing category immediately and obligatorily.

Other constituents that are immediately dominated by a mother node may be encountered before or after the MNCC. In either case they are

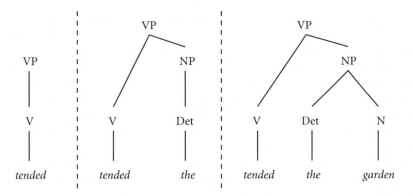

Figure 2.1. The stages in the construction of the verb phrase *tended the garden*. Notice that *tended* constructs the VP, and *the* constructs the NP. Attachments to the VP node start when *tended* is heard, and end when *the* is heard.

attached to the mother node as rapidly as possible after it has been constructed:

IC attachment. Immediate constituents that are discovered before the MNCC for a particular mother node are placed in a look-ahead buffer for non-constructing nodes. As soon as a mother node is constructed, all ICs (immediate constituents) that can be attached to the mother node in accordance to phrase structure rules are attached as quickly as possible, either by removal from the buffer or by being encountered later in the parse.

The human parser must obviously use more than just these two parsing mechanisms, but these two will be enough to motivate the parsing principle, early immediate constituent recognition (EIC).

The EIC metric

Early immediate constituent recognition (EIC) is the most important of Hawkins's parsing principles and provides a method of calculating a measure of parsing difficulty for a particular tree structure and a particular grammar. The basic idea behind the EIC is that of the constituent recognition domain (CRD) of a particular node.

Constituent recognition domain. The CRD for a node N is the ordered set of words in the string being parsed, starting from the MNCC of the first IC of N on the left to the MNCC of the last IC of N on the right and including all intervening words.

It is possible to attach all daughter ICs to a mother node on the basis of a subset of the words dominated by that mother node. It is this subset that is described by the CRD. So, for example, in the sentence *Brian hid under the tree*, all the ICs of the verb phrase may be attached after the words *hid under* have been parsed, since *hid* will construct VP, and *under* will construct PP, which is the last IC of the verb phrase. As we shall see in the next chapter, this concept of relevant subsets of structure can be generalized to other psycholinguistic operations. Given that the parser will prefer to recognize structure completely as rapidly as possible, it is logical to assume that there will be a preference for smaller subset structures—shorter CRDs. Notice that the definition of CRD makes no mention of the MNCC of the mother node itself. If this occurs at the right end of the string, then the daughter ICs, once constructed, will be placed in a look-ahead buffer as described above, and will be attached once the mother node is constructed at the end of the string—the concept of the CRD, therefore, holds wherever in the domain the mother node is actually constructed.

Evidence for the validity of CRD length as a measure of parsing complexity can be seen in particle movement in English. In Examples 2.4–2.6 below, the CRD of the verb phrase (marked by underbraces) is lengthened as the length of the noun phrase increases. Example 2.7, however, has a short CRD, since the noun phrase is the last daughter IC of the verb phrase and the determiner constructing the noun phrase marks the end of the CRD:

(2.4) Florence $_{VP}$[looked $_{NP}$[the phone number] up]

(2.5) Florence $_{VP}$[looked $_{NP}$[the phone number of her friend] up]

(2.6) Florence $_{VP}$[looked $_{NP}$[the phone number of her friend Dougal, whom she wanted to speak to] up]

(2.7) Florence $_{VP}$[looked up $_{NP}$[the phone number of her friend Dougal, whom she wanted to speak to]]

It is quite apparent that the acceptability of the sentences decreases as the length of the CRD increases. Hawkins (1994*a*) gives many more examples that suggest that rearrangement rules in various languages tend to work to decrease the length of the CRD.

A metric can be calculated to quantify this preference for short CRDs, and also to differentiate between CRDs of the same length to give preference to the CRD that gives information about constituency earlier in the left-to-right parse of the sentence. This metric reflects the parser's preference for the 'earliest possible temporal access to as much of the constituency information as possible' (Hawkins 1990: 233).

The EIC metric: the average of the aggregate left-to-right IC-to-word ratios of all the CRDs in the sentence.

Aggregate left-to-right IC-to-word ratio: the average of all IC-to-word ratios for each word in a particular CRD where the ratio for a word w_j in a CRD $[w_1 \ w_2 \dots w_n]$ dominated by an IC_i in a set of ICs $[IC_1 \ IC_2 \dots IC_m]$ is $\frac{i}{j}$.

For example, the aggregate left-to-right IC-to-word ratio for the VP in the phrase *tended the garden* can be calculated as follows. The CRD for the VP is: *tended the*. The first word is also in the first IC of the VP, so its IC-to-word ratio is $\frac{1}{1}$. The second word is also in the second IC, so its IC-to-word ratio is $\frac{2}{2}$. This gives us an aggregate ratio of 1, which is the best aggregate ratio that can be achieved for a constituent recognition domain. In other words, no reordering of the words *tended the garden* could make the VP easier to parse. We will see cases in the next section where there are suboptimal ratios, however.

I will not go into details of how Hawkins arrived at this method of calculation; suffice to say it in some way captures numerically the preference of the parser for access to as much constituency information as possible as quickly as possible within a particular 'parsing window'—the CRD. The purpose of this chapter is to examine what can be said about word-order universals *given* this metric. A different research topic could be the testing of the validity of this metric *as a reflection of parsing preference*, but, to keep within the scope of the chapter, I assume that Hawkins is correct on this point.

EIC and competence

The EIC metric can be used to make predictions about not only the rearrangement rules that might occur in performance, but also the basic orders found in the competence grammar. If we assume that the pressure from the parser will influence the word orders of the world's languages, we might expect to find the EIC metric for a particular construction to be reflected in the number of languages that allow that construction. Hawkins (1990: 236) calls this the *EIC basic order prediction* (essentially, a statement of fit):

EIC predicts that, in the unmarked case, the basic orders assigned to the ICs of phrasal categories by grammatical rules or principles will be those that provide the most optimal left-to-right IC-to-word ratios; for basic orders whose ratios are not optimal (the marked case), then the lower the ratio, the fewer exemplifying languages there will be.

Perhaps the most important prediction that the EIC principle allows us to make is that languages which have consistent left or right branching in binary tree structures will be more frequent than those that have inconsistent orderings. In the sentences below, the aggregate left-to-right ratio for the verb phrase is shown (each word's ratio is shown next to that word):

(2.8) Brian $_{VP}\left[\text{hid}_{\frac{1}{1}}\ _{PP}[\text{under}_{\frac{2}{2}}\ \text{the tree}]\right]$

$$\text{aggregate ratio} = 1$$

(2.9) Brian $_{VP}\left[_{PP}\ [\text{the tree under}_{\frac{1}{1}}]\ \text{hid}_{\frac{2}{2}}\right]$

$$\text{aggregate ratio} = 1$$

(2.10) Brian $_{VP}\left[_{PP}\ [\text{under}_{\frac{1}{1}}\ \text{the}_{\frac{1}{2}}\ \text{tree}_{\frac{1}{3}}]\ \text{hid}_{\frac{2}{4}}\right]$

$$\text{aggregate ratio} = 0.58$$

(2.11) Brian $_{VP}\left[\text{hid}_{\frac{1}{1}}\ _{PP}[\text{the}_{\frac{2}{2}}\ \text{tree}_{\frac{2}{3}}\ \text{under}_{\frac{2}{4}}]\right]$

$$\text{aggregate ratio} = 0.79$$

In each of these examples, the CRD of the verb phrase stretches from *hid* to *under* or vice versa, since these construct the two ICs of the verb phrase. The verb phrases of Examples 2.8 and 2.9 both have optimal CRDs because the MNCCs of the two ICs occur together. In general, for any binary branching tree, the optimal ordering in terms of the EIC metric will be that which *consistently* places MNCCs to the right or left of the non-constructing constituent (Figure 2.2). Since the head of a phrase is always an MNCC for that phrase, this seems to provide an explanation for the tendency for consistent head ordering across languages. The left-to-right nature of the EIC metric also predicts an asymmetry in *suboptimal* phrases. Example 2.11 has a higher metric than Example 2.10, reflecting the extremely low proportion of SOV languages that have prepositions.

This is just one example of how the EIC metric is reflected in the competence grammars of the world's languages. Many others are discussed in Hawkins (1994*a*).

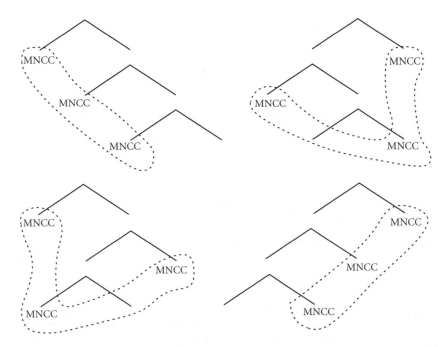

Figure 2.2. Some imaginary binary branching tree structures with MNCCs marked, showing the effect of different orderings on the length of CRDs (circled). Having the MNCCs consistently on the left or the right of the branching material means that the CRDs are shorter.

Selection and emergence

The explanation outlined in the previous section relies on an assumption—made explicit in the basic order prediction—that parsing complexity is directly reflected in the distribution of types of grammars in the world's languages. A sceptical viewpoint on this assumption gives rise to the *problem of linkage* discussed in Chapter 1. In this specific case, the problem of linkage is:

> How does a property of the human parser—namely the preference for early immediate constituent recognition—give rise to a restriction on the distribution of occurring languages in the space of possible languages—namely constraints on possible word orders in competence grammars?

To put it crudely, *even if* we have a theory of parsing that shows us that occurring languages are consistently less complex than non-occurring

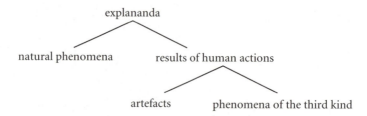

Figure 2.3. Keller's taxonomy of phenomena.

languages, we should still be puzzled and wonder, 'how is it that the languages we find so neatly dovetail with the design of our parser?' The answer to this question relies on the idea that languages can *adapt*; this section argues that this adaptation is effected by a type of linguistic selection.

Universals are phenomena of the third kind

Keller (1994) puts forward an *invisible-hand* account of language change. In this theory, language changes are viewed as *phenomena of the third kind*. Essentially, Keller gives us a typology of phenomena (Figure 2.3), dividing explananda into natural phenomena and results of human action; and further dividing the latter into artefacts, and phenomena of the third kind. These phenomena of the third kind can be characterized as those 'things which are the result of human actions but not the goal of their intentions' (Keller 1994: 56). The process that gives rise to these phenomena is termed the 'invisible-hand process'.

Keller discusses individual language changes as instances of objects of this kind. He gives as an example the change in the senses of the word *englisch* in German in the nineteenth century. In the early nineteenth century *englisch*$_1$ 'angelic' and *englisch*$_2$ 'English' were both used, but around the middle of the century the former disappeared. Keller points out that the explanation for this phenomenon must refer to the actions of users of the language, and yet cannot be said to have been their *goal*. The explanation for the change involves setting out the *ecological conditions* that users of German found themselves in at the time of the change; *maxims of action* that describe the behaviour of individual language users; and the *invisible-hand process* that gives rise to the non-local consequences of that behaviour (for details of this explanation, see Keller 1994: 93–5). The disappearance of *englisch*$_1$, in this view, is an *emergent property* of the interaction of the users of German at the time.

Universals are similarly non-intentional results of human action. In other words, the local, individual actions of many speakers, hearers, and

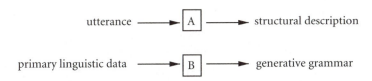

Figure 2.4. Chomsky's diagram showing the mechanisms involved in the perception and acquisition of language.

acquirers of language across time and space conspire to produce non-local, universal patterns of variation. A description of the invisible-hand process in this case is a theory of the propagation of variation through individuals. Indeed, the same mechanisms that explain individual language changes can be called upon to explain universals (although we are less interested in specific *ecological conditions*, as opposed to the universal pressures which will be relevant to each instance of change). A particular universal such as *SOV* & ¬*Pr* can be thought of as a *higher order emergent property*.

This brief discussion points to some desirable features we might look for in an explanation for universals. In particular, we should hope to make reference only to the actions of individuals at individual points in time. Furthermore, our model of the individual must describe precisely the relationship between these actions and the ecological conditions in which the individual is situated. The next section looks in more detail at this relationship, and discusses how language can persist from generation to generation in a population.

The arena of use

Chomsky (1964) characterizes general linguistic theory as an attempt to understand the nature of the boxes labelled A and B in Figure 2.4. It is worth quoting his description of this diagram in full:

The perceptual model A is a device that assigns a full structural description D to a presented utterance U, utilizing in the process its internalized generative grammar G, where G generates a phonetic representation R of U with the structural description D. In Saussurean terms, U is a specimen of *parole* interpreted by the device A as a 'performance' of the item R which has the structural description D and which belongs to the *langue* generated by G. The learning model B is a device which constructs a theory G (i.e., a generative grammar G of a certain *langue*) as its output, on the basis of primary linguistic data (e.g., specimens of *parole*), as input. To perform this task, it utilizes its given *faculté de langage*, its innate specification of certain heuristic procedures and certain built-in constraints on the character of the task to be performed. (Chomsky 1964: 26)

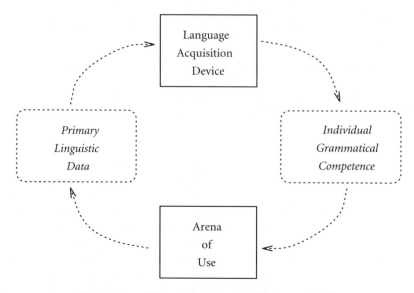

Figure 2.5. The cycle of acquisition and use.

Hurford (1987: 20–3), drawing on work by Andersen (1973), extends Chomsky's model of language acquisition (the lower half of Figure 2.4) by highlighting the fact that the PLD are themselves the output of another object, what he calls the 'arena of use', which in turn takes its input from grammars. Figure 2.5 shows Hurford's diagram. Both the innate LAD (Chomsky's 'B') and the arena of use play a part in *determining* language structure. Hurford (1990: 98, 100) describes the latter as follows:

The Arena of Use is where utterances . . . exist. The Arena of Use is a generalisation for theoretical purposes of all the possible non-grammatical aspects, physical, psychological, and social, of human linguistic interactions. Any particular set of temporal, spatial, performance-psychological and social coordinates for a human linguistic encounter is a point in the Arena of Use.

As for the usefulness of coining the expression 'Arena of Use', my purpose is to focus attention on a vital link in the transmission of language from one generation to the next.

Where should the parser (Chomsky's 'A'), or other processing mechanisms, be placed in this scheme? This depends crucially on a definition of 'primary linguistic data'. If PLD are taken to mean the linguistic data that the language learner hears, then the parser must sit on the arc between the PLD and the LAD. However, to say that the PLD are *linguistic* data is begging the question: how does the child filter out other acoustic information, such as coughs, whistling, or even foreign-language sentences?

Whatever the definition of PLD, some processing mechanism *must* exist in the arena of use to act as a filter. Some might argue that the LAD contains the necessary machinery to filter out non-linguistic data, but this explanation is unsatisfactory, since the same machinery must be used even after acquisition ceases, suggesting that it must be a separate module. The strong definition of PLD that I put forward is, therefore, *the data that a child attends to as linguistically salient*. All innate processing mechanisms can be distinguished from the LAD by the fact that they deal with a superset of the PLD. This superset of 'raw' data is filtered by the processing mechanisms to provide the PLD for the LAD. In fact, in order to dispel confusion, we might dispense with the term 'PLD' altogether and simply refer to *language data* and *trigger experience* for pre- and post-filtering linguistic data respectively. Lightfoot (1989: 324, 325) makes precisely this point in connection with learnability theory:

The trigger is something less than the total linguistic experience . . . the child might even be exposed to significant quantities of linguistic material that does not act as a trigger . . .

This means that children sometimes hear a form which does not trigger some grammatical device for incorporating this form in their grammar. Thus, even though they have been exposed to the form, it does not occur in mature speech.

Interestingly, arguing from a connectionist viewpoint, Elman (1991) also suggests that the trigger experience will be a subset of the total raw linguistic data. He shows that, for a connectionist model to learn a non-trivial grammar successfully, the data used for 'acquisition' must be presented in stages from simple to more complex. Consequently, his model initially incorporates a memory limitation which effectively filters out the more complex grammatical structures.

There are other logically possible means by which a parsing preference might make itself felt in the acquisition–use cycle. One could hypothesize that the human-language *generation* mechanisms are subject to similar considerations of syntactic weight as the parser and thus that the generation of sentences that are difficult to produce will be avoided. The nature of human-language generation is relatively poorly understood, but it has been suggested (e.g. Hawkins 1992c) that speakers may respond to considerationsof parsing efficiency since the primary goal of the speaker is effectively to communicate to a hearer. Hence the production of sentences that are hard to parse is avoided specifically for the reason that they will be difficult to understand. However, if the parser filters sentences from the acquisition–use cycle, then it is unnecessary to postulate this kind of speaker–hearer symmetry in order to model the influence of the parser on language change. These issues will be discussed later in this chapter.

Complex adaptive systems

Gell-Mann (1992) suggests that language change can be characterized as a complex adaptive system—that is, a system that evolves and shows evidence of emergent 'fit' for some function. The most well-known case of a complex adaptive system is biological evolution (although global economics, culture, and learning have all been studied in similar terms). Organisms clearly show evidence of fit with their environment, and this is explained by the theory of natural selection. Particular sequences of DNA persist from generation to generation by being expressed as organisms that successfully produce offspring. However, this persistence is not guaranteed, since not all organisms necessarily breed. Nature provides a *selective pressure* on sequences of DNA mainly by ensuring that only a subset of organisms will survive.

Gell-Mann points out that this selective effect is the central feature of complex adaptive systems. In the process of replication of information through these systems, selection provides a bottleneck that induces adaptation. In the biological case, since some individuals must die before breeding, the sequences of DNA that persist will necessarily be those that code for individuals that are more successful. Over time, the process of natural selection tends to produces organisms that are well adapted to pass through the bottleneck in the system.

How might the paradigm of complex adaptive systems be applied to language evolution on the historical timescale (what Hurford (1990) calls *glossogenetic* language evolution)? In other words, what is the equivalent bottleneck for transmission of information over time in the linguistic case? If we can set up a model for *linguistic* selection as opposed to *natural* selection, then we will have gone some way towards understanding the puzzle of fit posed in Chapter 1.

A good candidate for a bottleneck in glossogenetic language evolution is the arena of use. The arena contains many utterances produced by the many grammatical competences of the speech community. However, for the information encoded in these competences to survive to the next generation, these utterances must be used as triggers for acquisition. I have already said that trigger experience must be a subset of all the linguistic data in the arena of use and that the parser can be seen as a filter in this process. This means that the selective pressure on information coded in competence grammars is provided by the parser. Ultimately, this selective effect is related to parsing principles such as EIC.

So, if the parser is a filter between raw data and the trigger experience, then it is possible that only some of the orderings of a particular constituent that occur in the raw data will be acquired. In order for Hawkins's explanation to work in this context, the probability of a particular utterance being used for acquisition will be proportional in some way to its EIC metric. It is possible, then, that different orderings in performance can become *fixed* in the competence grammar, or, in a less extreme case, different orderings may become marked in some way.[3] The generalization is that *in the process of acquisition* the EIC metric may make itself felt by influencing the variability of word orders that the child learns. This argument is equivalent to one that claims that acquisition and language change are dependent on text frequency:

If . . . a parameter is not expressed frequently in the input text, the learner will be under less pressure to set that parameter in accordance with the target setting. In this case . . . either the correct setting or the incorrect setting can survive in the linguistic environment.   (Clark and Roberts 1993: 301)

The only modification here is to view the 'input text' as the input to acquisition *after* parsing.

It is likely that a particular ordering will not disappear suddenly from a language, so a sensible assumption is that the EIC metric changes the *frequency of use* of a particular ordering through the process described above. This seems to suggest that the child must learn, not only a particular construction, but a frequency as well. However, this assumption is not necessary for a description of gradual language change, if we define frequency of use of an ordering as being a reflection of a particular speech community's use of that ordering. In other words, it is possible to have different frequencies for different orders without compromizing a theory of 'all-or-nothing' competence. The frequency of use of a particular ordering by one generation is some function of the frequency of use of that ordering by the previous generation and the EIC metric of that ordering. I shall refer to this process, whereby a particular word-order pattern gradually becomes fixed in the competence grammar, as *grammaticalization*. This term has been used by a large number of scholars to refer to diverse linguistic phenomena (see e.g. Heine *et al.* 1991). Traugott and Heine (1991: 1), however, admit the use of the term in this case by defining it as 'that part of the theory of language that focuses on the interdependence of langue and parole, of the categorial and less categorial, of the fixed and less fixed in language'.

---

[3] There is a general problem of circularity involved in any filtering of the PLD that appeals to grammatical competence. Since the parser must make use of a competence grammar *in order* to provide input to the acquisition process, it is pertinent to ask how such a competence ever arises. Jim Hurford (personal communication) has suggested that this circularity can be avoided if acquisition is looked at *incrementally* in stages from primitive structures to more sophisticated.

Linguistic selection as transformation

To recap on the ground we have covered so far: the desirable features of an explanation that appeals to use have been set out by characterizing the explanation in terms of the invisible hand, and it has been argued that the influence of processing on language competence should be seen as a selective influence. More properly, functional pressures must influence the selection of linguistic variants that are *competing* in some way, and this selection must occur at some point in the cycle of language acquisition and use. Another way of seeing this is that there is a set of transformations that link diachronically the competence of a speaker at some point in time to the competence of a speaker in the same speech community at some later time. Critically, these transformations are not necessarily preservative. If they were, then there would be no language change. Furthermore, functional selection influences these transformations, and hence the survivability of features of languages, in a predictable, though statistical, manner.

Viewing linguistic evolution in terms of transformations between different types of object (here, competence and performance, or I-language and E-language), closely parallels biological thinking (as we should expect if biological evolution and linguistic evolution are both complex adaptive systems). So closely, in fact, that we can usefully borrow a map of transformations from Lewontin (1974, cited in Sober 1984), and replace *genotypes* with *I-language* and *phenotypes* with *E-language*. The first important feature to note about Figure 2.6 is that the transformation from competence to competence involves objects in two very different domains. The *I-language* domain contains objects in individual speakers' brains. The objects, the domain in which they exist and the transformation T4 (acquisition), are what Chomsky (1986) argues are the proper target of study in linguistics.

On the other hand, we have the *E-language* domain, which contains *utterances* in some broad sense. These objects are more ephemeral, and are typically viewed as epiphenomena in the Chomskyan programme. The transformation T2 involves features of the world at particular points in time—for example, the level of noise, the availability of hearers, and so on.

Finally, we have the transformations T1 and T3 which map objects in one domain to those in the other. The former is mediated by speakers (production), and the latter by hearers (parsing). Neither these transformations nor those that map between objects within domains are well understood by linguistic theory, but it is generally assumed that some innate (and therefore universally shared) neurological mechanisms play a role. In particular the focus of the explanation in this chapter is on the role of complexity of processing in influencing the transformation T3—in other words, the effect of EIC.

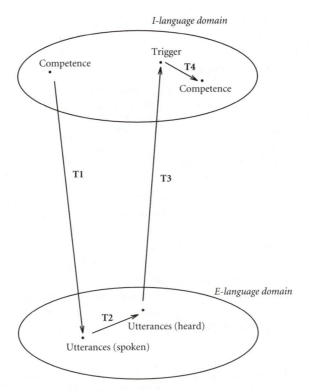

Figure 2.6. Transformations within and between *I-* and *E-domains.*

Replacement through competition and the notion of fitness

Given a simple case of two linguistic forms somehow in competition combined with the model outlined above, what might we expect to happen? Kroch (1989*a, b*) discusses the rise of periphrastic 'do' in English as a case of replacement of one form with another, so a brief review of his work will be useful in this context.

First, some terminology: given a linguistic form f carrying out some function M, f' is a *variant* form of f carrying out the same function M. The variants f and f' will typically occur as doublets historically and will be viewed as synonymous to native speakers.[4] Finally I will use $f > f'$ to mean that f is preferred in performance for some reason, and F or F' to signify a language type in which the form f or f' is *basic.*

---

[4] It is likely that these sorts of truly synonymous variant forms are actually uncommon, if they occur at all. Instead, variants will belong to a gradient scale of functional differentiation. This is a complex issue, to which we will return in Chapter 4.

Kroch (1994) refers to situations where languages change their relative frequency of variants as *grammar competition*. Under his formulation, syntactic doublets behave in the same way as morphological doublets in competition for a paradigm slot.

If we take this view seriously, we are led to the conclusion that syntactic variation should be governed by the same principles as variation in morphology, since the locus of the variability in the two cases is the same—the formative. Just as morphological variants which are not functionally distinguished are disallowed, so we should not expect to find variation between semantically non-distinct syntactic heads. To the extent that such variability is found, it poses the same theoretical problem as the appearance of doublets does in morphology.   (Kroch 1994: 5)

Kroch points out that the 'blocking effect' in morphology (whereby the presence of an irregular form in a paradigm slot blocks the occupation of that slot by a regular form) is a central tenet of modern morphology. However, doublets *are* in fact often observed in languages. If the doublets are functionally equivalent, speakers 'learn either one or the other form in the course of basic language acquisition, but not both' (p. 6). Later on the same speakers may recognize the existence of the variant form, which 'for them has the status of a foreign accent' (p. 6). Finally, one of these two doublets will tend to win out in a particular community—thus justifying our use of the term *competing variants*—or the two forms will become functionally differentiated.

Now, given the doublet forms f and f' where $f > f'$, we would expect the frequency of f in a speech community to increase over time. What

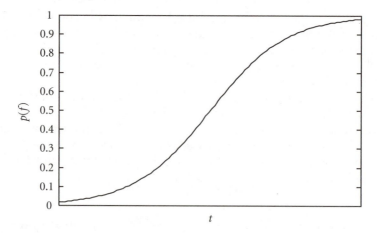

Figure 2.7. The time course of replacement through competition.

would the time course of such a change look like? Kroch (1989*b*) looks at the emergence of periphrastic 'do' in English between 1400 and 1575.

The basic fact of this case is that Middle English main verbs behave like auxiliaries in three word-order contexts: questions, negative sentences, and sentences with weak adverbs. In each of these contexts, Middle English main verbs give evidence of movement to a functional head above VP (INFL in the terminology of the relevant studies) while modern English main verbs do not. In modern English, the verb instead seems to remain within the VP, or at least in a position below the tense and subject-agreement functional head or heads. In questions and negative sentences, where the functional heads need lexical support, the periphrastic auxiliary 'do' appears.   (Kroch 1994: 2)

Two of the examples that Kroch gives to contrast the Middle English and Modern English usage are repeated here:

(2.12)   (a)   How great and greuous tribulations suffered the Holy Appostels?

   (b)   How great tribulations did the Holy Apostles suffer?

(2.13)   (a)   ... spoile him of the riches by sondrie faudes, whiche he perceiueth not.

   (b)   ... which he does not perceive.

   A quantitative analysis of texts which contain these variant forms show that the change (unsurprisingly) is not instantaneous. Instead, one form takes over from the other slowly at first, then more quickly until it has nearly taken over, at which point the rate of change slows once again. This shape of change fits well with a simple mathematical model given by Kroch (1989*b*):

$$p(f) = \frac{e^{k+st}}{1 + e^{k+st}}$$

where t is time, k is a constant determined by the initial frequency of f, and s is the slope parameter, related to the degree to which f is preferred to f' (see Figure 2.7). The shape of this function makes sense intuitively if one realizes that the rate of growth of a new form is related not only to the numbers of that form already about, but also to the number of forms to be replaced (the derivative of the function above is $sp(f)p(f')$). So, the slope on the left hand of the graph in Figure 2.7 is shallow since there are few fs about, and the right-hand slope is shallow since there are few f's left to replace. It is suggestive, in the light of arguments in the previous section, that the same *logistic* function is used in biology to map the replacement in a population of genetic alleles that differ in Darwinian fitness (Spiess 1989, cited in Kroch 1989*b*). The fit of observed *syntactic* changes to this function has been tested by Kroch (1989*b*) and shown to be good. This lends further weight to the suggestion above that syntactic as well as morphological change proceeds through a process of replacement by competition.

The next question that must be addressed is how to fit a performance theory like Hawkins's into a model of replacement through competition. Given the abstract example above, and all else being equal, a language of type F' will change over time into a language of type F. The manner in which f forms win out is by selection in **T3** because $f > f'$—in other words, f is preferred to f' in parsing. In general, we can define this preference in terms of *fitness*, where *fitness* is a function from frequency ratios of pairs of variants to the average probability of acquisition of those variants. Where there are only the two variants under consideration, a plot of fitness by variant frequency gives us a simple graph with fitness increasing as the frequency of f increases. For reasons that will become clear in the next section, this graph is referred to as a *fitness landscape* and languages, according to this theory, will tend to 'climb' these landscapes and maximize fitness. In other words, through a process of selection, they will organize themselves to maximize the chances that their variants will survive in the arena of use.[5]

It might now be clear that the role of a theory of parsing complexity such as John Hawkins's is to provide a description of fitness landscapes. This conception of functional pressures—the first step to solving the problem of linkage—will be useful in understanding the behaviour of a computer simulation of linguistic selection described in the next section.

A simulation of the complex adaptive system

In order to understand the implications of the model introduced in the previous sections, and to ensure that its details are completely explicit, computational simulations of the adaptive process can be constructed (for examples of this approach, see Hurford 1989, 1990; Werner and Dyer 1991; MacLennan and Burghardt 1993; Ackley and Littman 1994; Batali 1994, 1998; Cangelosi and Parisi 1996; Oliphant 1996, 1997; Oliphant and Batali 1996; Steels 1996, 1997; Briscoe 1997; Kirby and Hurford 1997*a*, *b*; Kirby 1998*b*, *c*). These simulations give us a way of experimenting with theory in some sense. A simulation of a theory in combination with a certain set of initial conditions can be used to see if the implications of the theory that we expect actually hold. Each run of the simulation can be seen as an

---

[5] Chapter 5 discusses exceptions to the general rule that languages will maximize their own fitness.

experiment—not with real languages or real language users, but with virtual languages and virtual users whose relevant characteristics are defined by the way in which the simulation is set up. In the case of complex adaptive systems, the use of computer simulation is particularly appealing, since emergent properties are expected to occur when many interacting virtual users are brought together—properties whose appearance may be hard to predict analytically. This is especially true of the simulations introduced in the next chapter. However, this section introduces a simple simulation of the linguistic selection of competing variants, and shows how the initial conditions can be set up which give rise to a behaviour characterized by the curve in Figure 2.7.

Components of the simulation

The simulation system which underlies the results in this chapter has the following simple components which correspond directly to parts of the model described above:

Utterances. These are the E-language domain objects in Figure 2.6. In the simulations described in this chapter, these utterances are not actual sentences, but simply types or features of sentences. So, for example, an utterance in this sense could be *SVO*, or *+coronal*, depending on what was being investigated.

Arena of use. In the simulations discussed here, this is an unstructured pool of utterances.

Grammars. These are the I-language domain objects in Figure 2.6. In the simulations in this chapter they are simply lists of possible *utterances*. A typical simple grammar might be *[SOV, NAdj]*. This is one possible idealization; another possible approach would involve the use of *parameters* to model I-language (see Niyogi and Berwick 1995).[6]

Speakers. The simulations start with a speech community which is made up of a set of speakers each of which consists of a grammar. These

---

[6] Niyogi and Berwick's (1995) recent paper analyses the dynamics of a system involving parametric variation. In particular they derive the S-shaped curve (a result identical to that independently arrived at by the simulation in this chapter). The main difference between their model and ours is that they do not assume that a probability distribution is imposed externally by linguistic selection. In the simplest case (involving one binary parameter), the change in two possible grammars is determined by the different distributions of sentences in the grammars' output which trigger either setting of the parameter. In this way Niyogi and Berwick appeal to features *internal to the I-domain* to derive the time-course of change (for further examples of the importance of the I-domain, see also the discussion in Chapter 4). A fascinating and important research project would combine Niyogi and Berwick's approach to parametric change, and the approach expounded here, to the fit of universals and processing.

grammars produce utterances for input to the arena in the way described below.

Acquirers.   These are speakers who have yet to be assigned grammars. They take input as utterances from the arena as described below.

It should already be obvious that the basic components of the simulation are gross idealizations of their real-world counterparts. This is just as it should be, however. The purpose of the simulation is not to be a complete analogue of the real world. Rather, it should be a reification of a theory. It should involve all the idealizations that a model of that theory would involve and only those idealizations. If we were to build a simulation of some theory of the flocking of birds, let us say, and we built in a detailed description of wind direction which the theory did not mention, then the results of the simulation would tell us nothing about the validity of our original theory. Of course, the process of building and testing the simulation might lead us to conclude that the original theory did not work *without* taking into account wind direction, but this simply serves to underscore the importance of simulation. Throughout this book there will be several cases where a theory will be shown to be inadequate through simulation in such a way.

The components listed above interact in the simulation according to two dynamic processes:

Production.   Speakers add utterances to the arena of use in line with their grammars. For the simulations in this chapter, this is done completely randomly.

Parsing/acquisition.   Acquirers become endowed with a grammar (and thus become speakers) in the following way:

1. A random subset of utterances in the arena of use is taken to form each acquirer's linguistic data.

2. This subset is then modified through a process of filtering to form a trigger experience. The process of filtering involves measuring the distribution of utterances in the linguistic data, and then choosing from those utterances in such a way that the probability of an utterance appearing in the trigger is related to its distribution and to its pre-defined parsing complexity.

3. The trigger is then directly mapped onto a grammar (i.e. if an utterance appears in the trigger, then it is added to the grammar).

A run of the simulation involves each speaker in the community producing some number of utterances to add to the arena, and then each acquirer parsing/acquiring utterances from the arena. The number of acquirers and speakers is always the same, so that, after acquisition, all the old speakers are discarded (as is the arena of use) and the acquirers become the new speakers for another iteration of the process.

A simple simulation: two competing variants

The details of the set-up of the simulation depend on the particular feature of interest. A simple simulation should make the process clearer. First, imagine a language with basic VO order and postpositions. According to Hawkins, such a language would suffer from a suboptimal EIC metric in structures such as $_{VP}[V_{PP}[NP\ P]]$, since the CRD for the verb phrase stretches across the noun phrase. Now, if a minor variant—prepositions—were introduced into that language, perhaps through language contact, then we would expect it to be preferentially selected from the arena of use by hearers because of its improved EIC metric. As a result, we would expect the frequency of prepositions in the arena to increase over time.

To test this with the simulation, the initial speech community was made up of 450 speakers with the grammar [*postp*] and fifty speakers with the grammar [*prep*]. To model the relative processing complexity of the variants, we need a way of preferentially selecting prepositions in the transformation between utterances heard by an aquirer and utterances that form part of the trigger experience. If we assume that the grammar of each individual can *only* be [*postp*] or [*prep*], then the aquisition process including selection can be modelled by:

(a) looking at the number of prepositions and postpositions in the input;

(b) converting these numbers into probabilities which reflect the chance of that variant being chosen at random from the sample to trigger acquisition;

(c) scaling these probabilities by using a complexity metric for the variants so that the probability of prepositions being used for acquisition is raised and the probability of postposition being used is lowered.

More formally, the manner in which each acquirer's trigger is selected from the linguistic data sampled from the arena of use[7] is governed by the

---

[7] The size of the sample was set to thirty utterances, which is large enough to give a fair approximation of the distribution of utterances in the arena without overly slowing the simulation down. The number of utterances allowed to each speaker is immaterial, since each speaker has only one possible utterance. This follows, since acquirers in this simulation could only acquire one variant.

following equations:

$$p(prep) = \frac{1.n_{prep}}{1.n_{prep} + 0.79.n_{postp}}$$

$$p(postp) = \frac{0.79.n_{postp}}{0.79.n_{postp} + 1.n_{prep}}$$

where $p(f)$ is the probability of the form f occurring in the trigger, n_f is the number of f forms in the linguistic data, and the values 1 and 0.79 correspond to EIC values for VO languages assuming a two-word NP (Hawkins 1990: 238). Any increase in the length of the NP would reduce the value of the postpositional EIC metric making any effect of the dispreference more marked. These equations can be thought of as the *fitness functions* for adpositions in VO languages.

The simulation was then run for thirty-five iterations, after which the arena of use consisted almost entirely of prepositions, the originally minor variant. The graph in Figure 2.8 shows the time course of the change (the vertical axis indicates the probability of finding a speaker with the

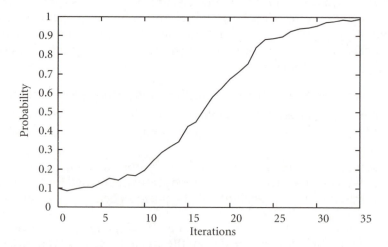

Figure 2.8. A simple run of the simulation showing VO&Postp changing to VO&Prep. The vertical axis shows the proportion of the population that has [*prep*] grammars. Initially this is set to be only 10%, but during the course of the simulation the proportion increases, following the time course also observed in real historical instances.

grammar [*prep*]). A striking feature of this graph is its similarity to the S-curve (Figure 2.7) which Kroch found in the historical data.[8]

The model in action

This section describes three further trials of the simulation which lend support to the theory put forward in this chapter. All the examples are adapted from Hawkins (1990, 1994*a*) and thus show how Hawkins's parsing theory in combination with a selection model of linguistic dynamics can explain the adaptive nature of various word-order universals.

Climbing a fitness landscape

In the example run of the simulation where a speech community adopted VO&Prep over VO&Postp, a function was described that mapped from relative frequency of adposition type to fitness. As the proportion of prepositions increases, so the average fitness of forms in the speech community increases. This fitness is simply an average of the probabilities of each form surviving to the arena of use at the next iteration. The process of adaptation through linguistic selection acts to maximize this fitness.

Now, consider a situation where the language of the speech community could vary along two dimensions, rather than one: for example, adposition order and verb–object order. This involves a modification to the grammars of the speakers in the simulation which may be either [*VO, Prep*], [*VO, Postp*], [*OV, Prep*] or [*OV, Postp*]. The state of the speech community at any one time can be expressed as a point in a two-dimensional space whose axes are the relative proportions of verb–object variants and adpositional variants. The interesting feature of this example is the way in which the fitnesses of the variants are related to each other.

The optimal orders in terms of parsing will be ones in which the heads (or, more correctly, MNCCs) are on the same side of their respective complements: in other words VO&Prep and OV&Postp. These are indeed what we find to be the most common orders in the world's languages. The parsing preference for prepositions over postpositions, then, is not absolute, but relative to the proportion of VO over OV in the arena of use, and vice versa.

To model this co-dependent relation we need once again to set up equations that weight the basic probability of finding a certain variant in the

---

[8] In fact, for this particular simple case, Clark (1996) proves mathematically that the equations governing selection described above *must* give rise to the logistic function that Kroch refers to. Clark shows, given certain idealizations about the size of the population, that the slope parameter in Kroch's model, s, is $\ln w_{prep} - \ln w_{postp}$ where w_{prep} is the complexity of prepositions and w_{postp} the complexity of postpositions. The initial constant, k, is $\ln p(prep) - \ln p(postp)$ at the start of the simulation.

input. However, whereas in the previous simulation the modifying weights (1 and 0.79) were fixed, here we cannot know the amount by which to bias a particular variant in advance. In other words, we cannot say, for example, that prepositions are preferred over postpositions. The basic form of the equations for each of the four variants Prep, Postp, VO, and OV will be the same as in the last example, then, except that the weights will be replaced by a general variable which we will need to calculate:

$$p(prep) = \frac{w_{prep}\, n_{prep}}{w_{prep}\, n_{prep} + w_{postp}\, n_{postp}}$$

$$p(postp) = \frac{w_{postp}\, n_{postp}}{w_{postp}\, n_{postp} + w_{prep}\, n_{prep}}$$

$$p(vo) = \frac{w_{vo}\, n_{vo}}{w_{vo}\, n_{vo} + w_{ov}\, n_{ov}}$$

$$p(ov) = \frac{w_{ov}\, n_{ov}}{w_{ov}\, n_{ov} + w_{vo}\, n_{vo}}$$

The weight variables w for a particular variant will be high if that variant is preferred, and the degree to which a variant is preferred is related to the numbers of the orthogonal variant in the arena at the time. For example, considering prepositions, the value of w_{prep} should be high if there are a lot of VO variants and few OV variants in the input, and low if the converse were true. The weight values for the variants are given by:

$$w_{prep} = \alpha\, n_{vo} + (1 - \alpha)\, n_{ov}$$

$$w_{postp} = \alpha\, n_{ov} + (1 - \alpha)\, n_{vo}$$

$$w_{vo} = \alpha\, n_{prep} + (1 - \alpha)\, n_{postp}$$

$$w_{ov} = \alpha\, n_{postp} + (1 - \alpha)\, n_{prep}$$

where α is some constant showing the relatedness of the two variant pairs, with $\alpha > 0.5$ signifying that prepositions and VO are positively correlated, and $\alpha < 0.5$ signifying that postpositions and VO are positively correlated.[9] The actual value of α will depend on the average length of noun phrases in the utterances spoken. For the simulation runs in this section, $\alpha = 0.6$.

[9] Notice that this assumes that the situation is symmetrical—in other words, that the preferred types VO&Prep and OV&Postp are equally preferred, and that the dispreferred types OV&Prep and VO&Postp are equally dispreferred. However, the EIC metric is not symmetrical in this case: VO&Postp is preferred to OV&Prep (Hawkins 1990: 238–9). The implications of this are explored in the next chapter.

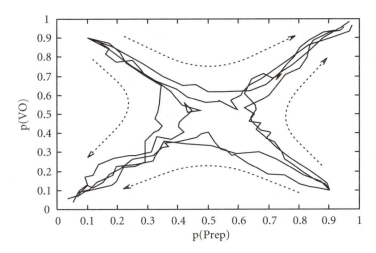

Figure 2.9. Eight runs of the simulation overlaid on the space of possible languages. The space is organized so that consistently prepositional and verb-initial languages are in the top-right corner, and consistently postpositional and verb-final languages are in the bottom left. The populations all start in an unlikely region of the space (i.e. VO&Postp or OV&Prep) and over the course of the simulation end up in one of the other two expected corners.

The simulation was run eight times; each run started with a population of 500 speakers, with mostly (i.e. 90 per cent) grammars that are uncommon in the world's languages. For half of the runs, the speakers mainly had the grammar [*VO, Postp*] and for half the runs [*OV, Prep*]. A plot of these runs is shown in Figure 2.9. The results are non-deterministic in that the language of the speech community ends up being either of the common cross-linguistic types, VO&Prep or OV&Postp, whatever the initial conditions.

We can see what is going on in this example by overlaying one of these runs on a plot of the function (for $\alpha = 0.6$):

$$F = \frac{w_{prep}\,n_{prep} + w_{postp}\,n_{postp} + w_{vo}\,n_{vo} + w_{ov}\,n_{ov}}{n_{prep} + n_{postp} + n_{vo} + n_{ov}}$$

This is the fitness function for the example. The function expresses the average weight score for all the variant forms in the community given a particular number of prepositions, postpositions, VO, and OV. The result is shown in Figure 2.10. It is clear from this figure that the simulation is climbing the fitness landscape. The important point of this graph is that

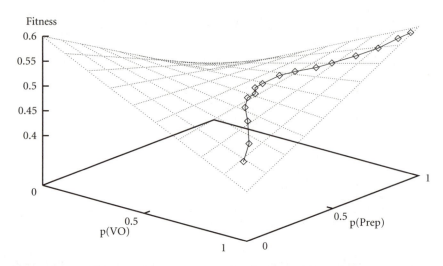

Figure 2.10. The simulation climbing a fitness landscape. High points on the landscape correspond to places in which the variants are preferred. Notice that the two peaks are the consistent head-ordering language types. The line corresponds to the movement of a particular speech community in the simulation over time as it climbs the landscape.

the peaks of the fitness landscape correspond to common cross-linguistic language types; the fitness landscape is described by a theory of parsing complexity; and speech communities climb fitness landscapes through a process of linguistic selection.

Multiple branching structures

The third example of the simulation in action involves a universal discussed in detail by Hawkins (1994*a*: §5.2.1) and tested by Kirby (1994: §4.1.2), involving the orders of noun, adjective, and relative clause in noun phrases. If the relative clause is comp-initial, then the noun and the adjective both precede the relative clause. English is an example of a language that has comp-initial relative clauses in which the adjective and noun precede the relative clause:

(2.14) *NP*[great music *S'*[that is played in the Cellar Bar]]

There are many languages with this ordering, and also a large number with a similar order but with the adjective and noun reversed.

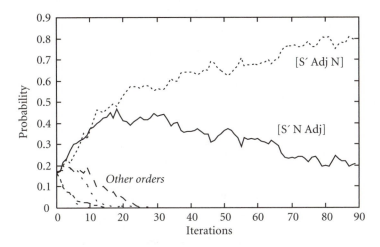

Figure 2.11. A run of the simulation with comp-final relative clauses. The initial population has equal numbers of all six possible orders; the two types that survive longest (with an initial relative clause) are the ones that are found cross-linguistically. Some of the other orderings survive for over twenty iterations.

If the relative clause is comp-final, on the other hand, then the noun and the adjective will probably both follow the relative clause, although there are a few exceptions (Hawkins lists Lushei, Dyirbal, Yaqui, and Hurrian) in which both precede. In no languages does the relative clause appear between the noun and the adjective as a basic order.

Once again, this set of facts seems readily explicable in terms of Early Immediate Constituents: the distance between the first and last of the three MNCCs of the ICs of the noun phrase (N, Adj, and Comp) is minimized. The worst cases are where the first MNCC is the first word of the clause and the last MNCC is the last in the clause.

The simulation was tested once assuming relative clauses were comp-initial, and once assuming they were comp-final. In each case there are six competing variants, their relative probabilities of making it into the child's trigger experience being determined by their EIC values (assuming a four-word relative clause). For these first runs, the initial speech community has equal numbers of each variant. The results, consistent with the universals above, are shown in Figures 2.11 and 2.12.

Notice that in the case of the comp-final relatives the alternative orderings last about twice as long as in the comp-initial case. This is because of an inherent left–right asymmetry in the calculation of the EIC metric. The

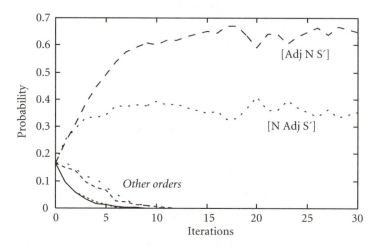

Figure 2.12. A similar run of the simulation with comp-initial relative clauses. Here, the two types that survive longest (with a final relative clause), are the ones that are found cross-linguistically. None of the other orderings survives over ten iterations.

best non-optimal orderings for comp-final relatives, $_{NP}[N \; Adj \;_{S'} [S \; Comp]]$ and $_{NP}[Adj \; N \;_{S'} [S \; Comp]]$, both have a metric of 0.81 (for a four-word relative clause), whereas the $_{NP}[Adj \;_{S'} [Comp \; S] \; N]$ and $_{NP}[N \;_{S'} [Comp \; S] \; Adj]$ orderings both work out at 0.68. As noted above, the exceptions to the relevant universals unsurprisingly involve the suboptimal orders for comp-final relatives. If the comp-final simulation is rerun with the optimal orders held at zero, the suboptimal orders eventually 'win out' over the worst orderings: $_{NP}[N \;_{S'} [S \; Comp] \; Adj]$ and $_{NP}[Adj \;_{S'} [S \; Comp] \; N]$. This is true even if the original state of the speech community is biased towards these non-occurring orders (Figure 2.13). This result suggests that a language that has $_{NP}[N \;_{S'} [S \; Comp] \; Adj]$, say, as its basic order will change its word order given any introduction of variation (except $_{NP}[Adj \;_{S'} [S \; Comp] \; N]$). This means that these worst-possible orders will not be likely to survive very long in any language, and this is reflected in the synchronic universals.[10]

---

[10] This raises some interesting questions about the origin of variation—the other side of the coin as regards a selectionist explanation. These issues are not covered in depth in this book; however, we can imagine a language-contact situation which would introduce a minor variant into a speech community. The important point is that, given multiple competing variants, it is possible that the optimum variant may not be available for selection, in which case the 'next-best' suboptimal variant may be selected. Of course, the chances of this happening (and the length of time such a variant survives) will be dependent on the parsing complexity of that variant, as shown here.

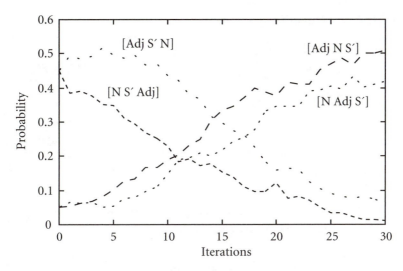

Figure 2.13. Suboptimal orders in a comp-final language. The initial population has neither of the optimal (relative-clause-initial) orderings, and has the two worst orderings much more frequently in the initial mix. Even in this case, the two suboptimal (but not worst) orderings with the relative clause in final position do take over.

These results also raise the question of what happens when two variants are equivalent in terms of parsing complexity (as are the optimal orders in these examples). The simulation does not converge on a single outright winner in a reasonable time. Instead, one order is stable as a minor variant. From this we might predict that wherever there are variant forms of equivalent processing complexity there will always be stable variation. However, this would be a mistake. Labov (1972), for example, discusses a case (the famous Martha's Vineyard study) of a particular sound change in which one variant form clearly wins out over another, even though there is no clear processing advantage. Instead, the change must be understood in sociolinguistic terms. Briefly, one form is considered the prestige variant and it is this asymmetry that drives the change (for discussion of this example in terms of selection, see also McGill 1993). Which particular form becomes the prestige variant in this and other such cases is arbitrary with respect to the form itself. So, although sociolinguistic considerations such as these are crucial for understanding change from a microscopic point of view, they do not inform an explanation of universals. We can imagine one of the optimal orders in the simulations above winning out by becoming associated with some sociolinguistic variable, but, since the

Table 2.1. *Word order of noun-modifiers*

$_{PP}[P \, _{NP}[Adj \, N]]$	$_{PP}[P \, _{NP}[NP \, N]]$	$_{PP}[P \, _{NP}[S' \, N]]$	Exemplifying languages
−	−	−	Masai
+	−	−	Greek
+	+	−	Maung
+	+	+	Amharic

process of association is arbitrary, we can assume that a particular form will be grammaticalized 50 per cent of the time.[11]

The prepositional noun-modifier hierarchy

The final example in this chapter is somewhat different from the others since it involves pairs of variants whose fitness is independent of each other. The pairs are noun–adjective order, noun–genitive modifier order, and noun–relative-clause order within NP. These form a hierarchical universal, the prepositional noun-modifier hierarchy (PrNMH) (Hawkins 1983):

> In prepositional languages, within the noun-phrase, if the noun precedes the adjective, then the noun precedes the genitive. Furthermore, if the noun precedes the genitive, then the noun precedes the relative clause.

$$Prep \rightarrow (NRel > NGen > NAdj) \text{ or} \ldots$$
$$Prep \rightarrow (AdjN > GenN > RelN) \text{ (the contrapositive hierarchy)}$$

Table 2.1 gives the combinations of structures that should be found cross-linguistically (where each row is a possible language, and a cross means that the language has that structure).

Furthermore, according to Hawkins's sample, languages can have mixed types. So, a language may have both NMod order and ModN order for a particular modifier. If so, then all the modifiers higher on the hierarchy will

[11] One angle for future research might be to see how often this type of selection becomes relevant. In this way it might be possible to predict the frequency of cases where a minor variant survives for an appreciable time. The symmetry of the two optimal variants cross-linguistically will always be preserved, however, as long as sociolinguistic selection has an arbitrary connection to form.

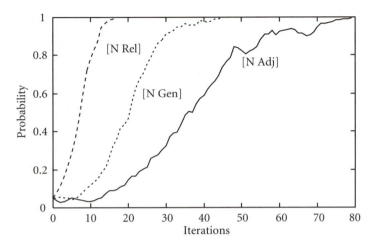

Figure 2.14. Change over time of three independent variant pairs. Each line represents the degree to which the language in the community has a postnominal modifier for each of relative clauses, genitives, and adjectives. Notice that all three lines follow the S-shaped time course, but at rates that correspond to the lengths of the modifiers, and hence their relative acceptibility to the parser.

appear to the left of the noun and all the structures lower on the hierarchy will appear to the right (e.g. French: AdjN/NAdj, NGen, NRel, or English: AdjN, GenN/NGen, NRel).

How can EIC make sense of these observations? Hawkins (1994*a*) shows that the EIC metrics of the structures decline down the hierarchy if the lengths of the preposed constituent *increase* down the hierarchy. Recall that consistent ordering of MNCCs is optimal for parsing. Given a prepositional language, we should expect the noun (the MNCC for the noun phrase) to be preferred as close as possible to the preposition—in other words, to the left of the modifier. The degree to which a structure will be dispreferred will depend on the distance that a postposed noun is away from the preposition. Hawkins argues that the typical length of relative clauses is greater than that of genitive modifiers, which in turn is greater than that of adjectives. The simulation takes the length of Adj to be 1 word, Gen to be 2 words, and Rel to be 4 words. The result is shown in Figure 2.14. (Notice that the initial situation is set to be at one end of the hierarchy. Kirby (1994) suggests that this could occur if a consistently head-final language changed its adposition order. There may be some problems with this, however, which will be discussed further in the next chapter.)

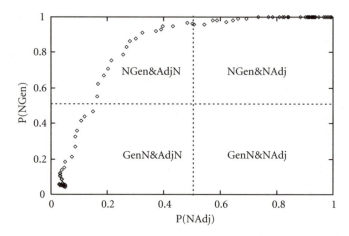

Figure 2.15. Plot of the simulation on NAdj/NGen space. Each point describes the state of the speech community in terms of the relative proportions of pre- and post-modifying adjectives and of pre- and post-modifying genitives. Notice that one of the four quadrants is not entered by the simulation in this plot.

Another way of visualizing these same results will show the implicational hierarchy more clearly. Figures 2.15 and 2.16 show the various states of the speech community over the course of the run. The four quadrants of the graph are labelled by language type assuming that the *conventional moment* (the point in time where a speech community is regarded as changing its grammatical conventions) occurs when the probability of a form is greater than 0.5. The quadrants which are not entered by the simulation are GenN&NAdj and RelN&NGen, exactly the types predicted not to occur by the implications underlying the PrNMH: *GenN* → *AdjN* and *RelN* → *GenN*.

Finally, if a prepositional language has two basic orders for a particular modifier in noun phrases, then it is likely that it is this modifier that is in the process of being preposed. If we arbitrarily section off part of Figure 2.14 around the 0.5 probability line as the area where we might expect free word order for a constituent, then the second typological observation is supported. If the area we choose is between 0.4 and 0.6, say, then, after five iterations, the speech community has the types AdjN, GenN, RelN/NRel; after twenty iterations, AdjN, GenN/NGen, NRel; after thirty-five, AdjN/NAdj, NGen, NRel.

The simulation results in this section show that the selection model can, in conjunction with his performance metric, lend support to Hawkins's basic order prediction, derive the S-shaped logistic curve, and provide

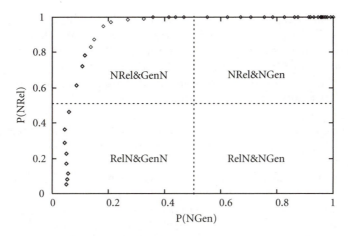

Figure 2.16. A similar plot of the simulation on NGen/NRel space. Notice, again, that one of the four quadrants is not entered by the simulation in this plot.

a simple explanation for the facts relating to the PrNMH (though see the discussion in Chapter 3). Of course, this does not demonstrate that Hawkins's theory is correct; in a sense the argument is a methodological one, demonstrating that viewing language as a complex adaptive system solves the problem of linkage. The remainder of this chapter looks at some of the further implications of adopting this position.

Unifying markedness correlates

As mentioned earlier, Matthew Dryer (e.g. Dryer 1992) uses a method of discovering statistical universals involving counts of *genera* (genetically related language groups of a time depth no greater than 4,000 years) grouped geographically, which is intended to compensate for genetic and areal bias.

On the basis of this improved method of gathering word-order correlations, Dryer argues against the generalization that *heads* tend to order consistently on one side or other of their dependents. Instead he demonstrates that it is *branching direction* that is relevant:

Branching Direction Theory (BDT): ... a pair of elements X and Y will employ the order XY significantly more often among VO languages than among OV languages if and only if X is a nonphrasal category and Y is a phrasal category.
    (Dryer 1992: 89)

Dryer points out that this theory is, in the main, consonant with Hawkins's EIC predictions, which prefer consistently left- or right-branching structures. The main difference is that BDT makes weaker predictions than EIC, which includes predictions about left–right asymmetries. These asymmetries should be investigated more closely using Dryer's statistically less biased method.

For our purposes, Dryer's BDT is suggestive of the way in which the adaptive model might be applied to the explanation of why certain criteria for markedness tend to correlate, not only with respect to word order, but in other domains also.

Given a universal of the type $P \rightarrow Q$ we may say that P is *marked* with respect to Q. This leads us to expect a cluster of linguistic properties associated with markedness to be manifested by P to a greater extent than by Q. Some of these properties as claimed in the literature are listed below:

Structural: the more marked value of a grammatical category will be expressed by at least as many morphemes as the less marked category. (Croft 1990: 73)

Behavioural (cross-linguistic): if the more marked value occurs in certain language types, then the less marked category will occur in at least those types. (Croft 1990: 83)

Frequency (textual): if the more marked value occurs with a certain frequency in a text sample, then the less marked value will occur with at least that frequency. (Croft 1990: 85)

Acquisition: the more marked value will be acquired later in child language acquisition than the less marked value. (Witkowski and Brown 1983: 569)

Language change: the more marked value will be added later and lost sooner than the less marked value in language change. (Witkowski and Brown 1983: 569)

The structural criterion for markedness is identified by Greenberg (1966: 26), following Jakobson's earlier work, as *zero expression*:

An important further characteristic of the marked/unmarked opposition ... I shall refer to ... as zero expression of the unmarked category. ... Thus parallel to the example *man* (unmarked), *woman* (marked), we have *author* (unmarked), *authoress* (marked) in which *author* indicates either a writer regardless of sex or specifically a male writer, whereas *authoress* designates only a female writer. In this latter instance the unmarked term *author* has a zero where the marked term *authoress* has an overt affix *-ess*. (Greenberg 1966: 26–7)

Notice that Greenberg is essentially defining structural markedness in terms of the *number* of morphemes in an expression. Croft notes that this means that the structural criterion is not a particularly useful one.

It is the best-known criterion for markedness in typology. Nevertheless, it is actually of somewhat limited application—for example, we cannot say which of the word orders RelN or NRel is marked on structural criteria—and possibly cannot be applied to phonology. Hence, it is a mistake to identify markedness solely with structural markedness.   (Croft 1990: 72–3)

This raises the question: can structural markedness be extended to include more than simply the number of morphemes? Here, the inclusion of *complexity* as a markedness criterion in Witkowski and Brown (1983) is the key. If a higher number of morphemes is a reflection of an increase in morphological *complexity*, then perhaps the *configuration* of those morphemes is also a factor in that complexity and hence a candidate for signalling markedness.

I propose, then, that the structural criterion for markedness may be extended to include word order:

> **Structural markedness (configuration):** if the more marked value involves a structure with a certain degree of branching coherence, then the less marked value will involve at least as high a degree of coherence.

Some explanatory remarks are in order here. Branching coherence refers to the extent to which a structure is consistently left- or right-branching, hence the structures $_a[_b[_c[\gamma\ \delta]\ \beta]\ \alpha]$ and $_a[\alpha\ _b[\beta\ _c[\gamma\ \delta]]]$ are maximally coherent whereas $_a[\alpha\ _b[_c[\gamma\ \delta]\ \beta]]$ and $_a[_b[\beta\ _c[\gamma\ \delta]]\ \alpha]$ are minimally so. The word 'involve' in this definition is problematic because the markedness of, say, NRel over RelN cannot be judged without examining the context of these structures. In other words, in VO languages NRel is less marked than RelN, but in OV languages the reverse in true. This is an example of *markedness reversal.*[12]

If branching coherence reflects parsing preference, as Dryer believes and Hawkins's theory predicts, then the adaptive model correctly predicts that the various criteria listed above will correlate. For example, an adpositional phrase within a verb-initial verb phrase may have two orders: $_{VP}[V\ _{PP}[P\ NP]]$ or $_{VP}[V\ _{PP}[NP\ P]]$. The latter of these orders is structurally marked with respect to the former because of its mixed branching—it is also harder to parse by Hawkins's EIC. These two possibilities

---

[12] Croft (1990: 135) points out that this general phenomenon has been called by various names in the literature, such as *local markedness* (Tiersma 1982) and *markedness assimilation* (Andersen 1972).

correspond to the graph in Figure 2.8. If the points on the graph correspond to possible human languages,[13] then the *frequency* and *behavioural* criteria apply. Furthermore, if we imagine a language in transition between points on the graph, then the *language change* criterion follows. Finally, although there is no explicit discussion of order of acquisition within the model, we may expect a form which is filtered out of the acquisition–use cycle more often to be successfully acquired later than a form that is not.

The assumption of speaker altruism

We have seen from the computer simulations in this chapter that combining Hawkins's performance theory with a theory of linguistic selection goes a lot of the way towards an explanation for word-order universals viewed as phenomena of the third kind. By assuming that the effect of parsing complexity is to influence the transformation of language data into trigger experience (transformation **T3** in Figure 2.6) we have a mechanism for solving the problem of linkage. A sensible question to consider at this point is what all this effort has bought us—what does this model add to the explanations in Hawkins 1994*a* apart from the various goals set out in Chapter 1? The main point on which this work differs from Hawkins's is connected with the role of the speaker in explanation. In line with Occam's Razor, the selection model so far has not had to call on the speaker to explain the adaptedness of languages, since hearer selection is enough. Hawkins, however, implicitly makes use of what I will call *the assumption of speaker altruism*.

For example, in Hawkins (1994*a*: 435) we find:

[Implicational] hierarchies define the sequence in which grammatical variants are selected within each grammatical domain, and the claim is being made that this sequence involves increasing complexity, and that the cut-off points represent a conventionalized response by speakers of each language not to tolerate processing difficulty or inefficiency below that point.

This suggests that the link between processing and competence grammars is the speaker. However, the complexity metrics discussed by Hawkins are measures of *parsing* complexity. If the locus of explanation is the speaker, this suggests that she is responding to the needs of the hearer in her choice of utterance. As Hawkins (1994*a*: 426) puts it, 'there is, of course, a general benefit for the producer if his or her speech is optimally packaged for the hearer, since communication will then be effective.' For this to be the case,

---

[13] This is a rather crude assumption which needs further justification in this case, as will be argued in the next chapter.

however, the speaker must calculate at each choice point in production the *parsing* complexity of the string about to be produced. Now, this may indeed be what is happening—our knowledge of the mechanisms of production is not such that we can know for certain at the moment—but, in the light of the explanation put forward, we can afford to be agnostic on this point.

Levelt's (1989) useful review of the experimental evidence relating to production puts forward a *modular* view of the production process that casts further doubt on the assumption of speaker altruism. He breaks the process down into two main stages: *conceptualization* and *formulation.* The first stage involves the intentional construction of a *preverbal message* which requires information from a discourse model, situational knowledge, and so on. This message is passed to the second stage, which constructs a *phonetic plan.* Crucially, given the modular approach, the mapping from message to phonetics is non-intentional and does not have access to situational knowledge.

Grammatical encoding takes a message as input and delivers a surface structure as output. It is likely that this process is highly automatic and non-intentional. A speaker will not, for every message, consider which of various grammatical alternatives would be most effective in reaching some communicative goal. (Levelt 1989: 282)

So, even if one of the speaker's communicative goals is to present utterances that are easy to parse, it is not possible that this can affect the choice of grammatical alternatives. To put it another way: to the extent that the preverbal message contains information about the intended order of presentation of a phonetic plan, the choice of a particular order cannot be responsive to the final syntactic form. The conceptualizer therefore cannot make EIC calculations, and the formulator will not be responsive to the needs of the hearer.

However, Levelt's model also includes a monitoring system whereby phonetic plans may be parsed by the speaker and fed back to the conceptualizer. That this self-monitoring is going on is clear from data on speech errors and corrections. Levelt (1989: 460–3) gives some examples that suggest this might be a way for speaker altruism to get in by the back door, so to speak. For example, when expressing a path through a set of coloured circles in one experiment, a speaker made the following 'repair' (from Levelt 1983):

(2.15) We go straight on, or—we enter via red, then go straight on to green.

Here, the speaker makes an error in the ordering of the two clauses, which express the sequence of actions to be made in an iconic fashion. This error appears to be caught by the speaker's own parsing mechanisms, which signal the need for a repair to the conceptualizer. Another example of word-order repair is (from Fay 1980):

(2.16) Why it is—why is it that nobody makes a decent toilet seat?

Again, self-monitoring signals the need for a repair, although in this case the speaker is aware of a syntactic error in the ordering of the subject and copula. Although these repairs seem to offer us a mechanism by which speakers can be responsive to the needs of hearers, it should be noted that all the examples given by Levelt are responses to *errors* rather than hard-to-parse outputs. 'Do speakers actually attend simultaneously to all these aspects of their speech? This is most unlikely, and there are data to support the view that . . . much production trouble is not noticed by the speaker' (Levelt 1989: 463).

Another possibility is that the pressures on language production (i.e. formulation) are simply the same as those on parsing. For such a story to work, speakers would have to prefer to 'build' constituent structure as rapidly as possible. So, a preference for minimal constituent production domains is predicted in parallel with the hearer's preference for minimal recognition domains. The problem with this approach is that the information available to speakers and hearers is radically different, so, when producing a verb-final verb phrase, the speaker *already knows* that a verb-phrase node can be constructed, whereas the hearer must wait for the MNCC, the verb. Thus this speaker-oriented approach fails to predict the structure of languages such as Japanese (Hawkins 1994a: 426).

It would, therefore, seem safer to try to formulate a solution to the problem of linkage that does not assume speaker altruism, and this has been the goal of this chapter. The next chapter returns to the role of the speaker in explaining language universals, though it will be argued not that speakers are altruistic, rather that their preferences are in direct conflict with those of hearers.

3 Hierarchies and Competing Motivations

The previous chapter examined a solution to the problem of linkage in the domain of word-order universals, using Hawkins's metric of processing complexity as an example of a partial explanation. This chapter extends the scope of the linguistic selection approach by examining an implicational hierarchy in another domain—accessibility to relativization.[1] Once again, Hawkins (1994a) provides us with a plausible explanation for the cross-linguistic facts in terms of structural complexity, and this will be the starting point for an investigation of the origins of hierarchies in general.

Relative clauses and structural complexity

The particular hierarchy which this chapter examines in depth was described some time ago by Keenan and Comrie (1977) in an important paper. They show that the accessibility of noun phrases to relativization depends on the grammatical function of the gap, or resumptive pronoun, within the relative clause. They define a hierarchy:

Subject > Direct Object > Indirect Object > Oblique
> Genitive > Object of Comparison

The following English examples exemplify each of these relative clause types in turn:

(3.1) the band that plays in the Jazz Joint [Subject]

(3.2) the band that I saw in the Jazz Joint [Direct Object]

(3.3) the band that I gave five pounds to [Indirect Object]

(3.4) the band that I play guitar in [Oblique]

(3.5) the band whose songs are funky [Genitive]

(3.6) the band that few are bigger than [Object of Comparison]

---

[1] The majority of this chapter appears as Kirby (1997).

This relative-clause accessibility hierarchy (AH) constrains possible languages according to the following definitions and constraints:

Subject relative universal. 'All languages can relativize subjects' (Comrie and Keenan 1979: 652). (A strategy that can relativize subjects is a *primary strategy*.)

Accessibility hierarchy constraints

1. 'If a language can relativize any position on the AH with a primary strategy, then it can relativize all higher positions with that strategy' (Comrie and Keenan 1979: 653).

2. 'For each position on the AH, there are possible languages which can relativize that position with a primary strategy, but cannot relativize any lower position with that strategy' (Comrie and Keenan 1979: 653).

Keenan and Hawkins (1987) report results from a psycholinguistic experiment testing native English speakers' ability to process relative clauses (RCs) at different points on the AH. The experiments were designed to test repetition of RCs that occurred modifying subjects in the matrix clause, so no conclusions can be drawn about: (*a*) other languages, (*b*) RCs modifying matrix objects etc., or (*c*) whether the AH affects production, or perception, or both. These points aside, the mastery of RCs clearly declined down the AH. As Keenan and Hawkins point out, this processing difficulty might explain the AH. Other experiments have been carried out that have tested the relative processing difficulty of RCs on the first two positions of the hierarchy (subject and direct object). MacWhinney and Pleh (1988) review a number of studies in comprehension in English children that are consistent with the view that subject relatives are easier to parse than object relatives (though see Chapter 4 for further discussion). Furthermore, their own study of Hungarian reveals a similar pattern.

Hawkins's (1994*a*) explanation of this universal relies on these claims that the ease of parsing of relative-clause constructions decreases down the hierarchy, and that this leads to the implicational constraints on crosslinguistic distribution. His suggestion is that languages somehow select a point on a hierarchy of parsing complexity below which relative clauses will be grammatical, and above which they will be ungrammatical (this approach, then, involves the implicit assumption of speaker altruism). What Hawkins adds to the work summarized above is an independent theory of structural complexity from which the parsing results can be derived.

The theory is related to EICs in that it defines a measure of tree-complexity associated with a particular node in a constituent that is relative to a particular psycholinguistic operation. In this case this operation is relativization, rather than constituent recognition. The complexity of relativization—or rather, processing a relative clause—is proportional to the size of a portion of the tree that is involved in co-indexing the trace, or pronoun, in the clause with its head noun. Hawkins's definitions (1994*a*: 28–31) are as follows:

Structural complexity of relative clause. The structural complexity is calculated by counting the nodes in the *relativization domain*.

Relativization domain. The relativization domain consists of that subset of nodes within the noun phrase dominating the relative clause that structurally integrate the trace or pronoun.

Structural integration of a node X in C. The set of nodes which structurally integrate X in C are:

- all nodes dominating X within C (including C itself);
- all[2] sisters of X;
- all sisters of the nodes dominating X within C.

The intuition captured by this definition is that relating the head noun with a trace (or pronoun) becomes more complex the more the trace (or pronoun) is embedded within the subordinate clause.

Hawkins demonstrates this metric using tree structures that rely on traditional notions of constituency, but the complexity rankings seem to remain the same if they are calculated using other syntactic analyses. Consider the structures in Figures 3.1 and 3.2, which are standard treatments of relative clauses within the principles and parameters tradition. The first tree is a structure where the subject (determiner phrase, or DP) situated in the specifier node dominated by the inflection phrase (IP) has moved to the specifier node dominated by the complementizer phrase (CP). This, then, is the structure of a subject relative. The nodes that are involved in the calculation of complexity are circled. The second tree is the equivalent for an object relative—in this case, it is obvious that the relative-clause complexity is higher. Similar arguments can be made for the relative ranking of other positions on the accessibility hierarchy (Hawkins 1994*a*: 39–41).

---

[2] In fact, some sisters may be excluded from the calculation if the language has flatter configurational structure. In this case, morphological case contributes to the calculation of structural complexity. For example, in languages without VPs, nominative marked NPs may be included as sisters of an accusative, but not vice versa. See Hawkins (1994*a*: 27–8) for discussion.

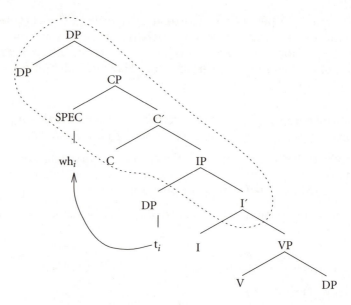

Figure 3.1. The tree structure of a subject relative.

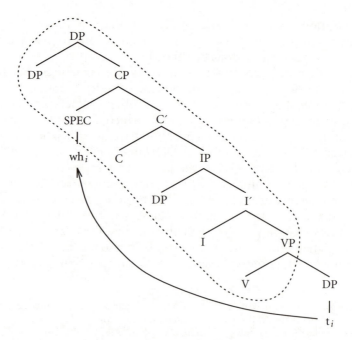

Figure 3.2. The tree structure of an object relative.

This account is successful in as much as it predicts the relative ranking of relative clauses in a hierarchy of parsing complexity, and uses concepts—such as structural domains—which can be generalized to other domains (e.g. word order and extraction). However, the theory as it stands does not answer the problem of linkage; exactly how do the structural complexity facts end up being expressed cross-linguistically? The next section attempts to answer this question in the same way as in the previous chapter, and in doing so shows that structural complexity *cannot on its own* give rise to hierarchy.

Extending the computational model

The simulation approach used here is almost identical to that of the previous chapter; the only real change is in the structure of the arena of use. So far, the simulations have been used to examine the time course of changes in a speech community. These have all resulted in a reduction of variation over time, leading eventually to a homogenization of the community—this has been referred to as grammaticalization of one of a set of variant options. In the case of the parametric universal relating the order of verb and object with adposition, we confirmed that the selection model made the right predictions by running the simulation several times and seeing what the end states were (half the time VO&Prep, half the time OV&Postp). It would be more satisfying, however, if the expected range of variation was reflected directly in the end state of the simulation. In other words, it would be preferable if the simulation did not always converge on one particular language type.

The element in the simulations that gives rise to homogenization seems to be the arena of use. All speakers input to an unstructured arena, and all hearer/acquirers take input from random points in the arena. Thus any differences in a population of speakers will be 'averaged-out' in the next iteration of the simulation. For there to be a stable end state with multiple types it must be possible for structure to emerge and be sustained in the population. The simulation described below achieves this by arranging speakers spatially and dividing the arena of use into many overlapping, localized arenas.

A new simulation

The simulations discussed here examine only the first two positions on the accessibility hierarchy—subject and direct object. Discussion in later sections shows how these results are easily extended to the rest of the hierarchy, and provide an explanation for the subject relative universal that we will ignore for the moment. The relevant components of the simulation are:

Utterances. The E-domain objects of the simulation. These may be either S, O, S', or O', corresponding to utterances with subject relatives, with object relatives, without subject relatives, and without object relatives.

Arena of use. A two-dimensional toroidal[3] space of utterances arranged such that an utterance at coordinates (x, y) was uttered by a speaker at (x, y).

Grammars. These are the I-domain objects. They are either SO, $S'O$, SO', $S'O'$ corresponding to the four possible language types.

Speakers. A speech community is made up of a two-dimensional toroidal space of speakers each of which consists of a grammar.

Acquirers. These are speakers without grammars. They take input from nearby coordinates in the arena (as described below).

The dynamic processes involved are:

Production. Speakers add utterances at random to the point in the arena at the same coordinates as themselves in line with their grammars.

Parsing/acquisition. Acquirers become speakers in the following way:

1. The neighbouring speakers' coordinates are found, where an acquirer has four neighbours: one above, one below, one to the left, and one to the right of its position.

2. All the utterances from the arena at the neighbours' positions and at the position of the acquirer are pooled together and a random subset is taken to form the linguistic data input to acquisition.

3. These data are filtered to form a trigger. This process involves measuring the relative distribution of variants in the data, and then choosing from those variants in such a way as to reflect its distribution and its relative structural complexity.

4. The trigger is then mapped directly onto the acquirer's grammar.

---

[3] A 'toroidal' space can be visualized as a square grid of cells such that a cell in the space has neighbours above, below, to the left, and to the right. The space is a torus if the square has no real edges—a cell on the bottom edge of the space has a neighbour at the top and vice versa, and a cell on the left edge has a neighbour on the right edge and vice versa. This geometry is chosen mainly because it is easily implemented, and because edges may introduce epiphenomenal effects which we are not interested in.

As with the simulations in the previous chapter, a run involves each speaker producing some number of utterances, and then each acquirer parsing/acquiring on the basis of the arena (although with this simulation the relevant data will be those produced 'nearby' the acquirer). After acquisition, the old speakers and arena are discarded and replaced by the acquirers, and the process is repeated.

Testing the explanation

If the explanation of the accessibility hierarchy based on a parallel hierarchy of structural complexity is correct, we should be able to run the simulation and see the implicational universal $O \rightarrow S$ emerge. In order to test this, the simulation is set up in a very similar fashion to the word-order experiments in the previous chapter. Two equations are needed that govern the probability of acquiring subject relatives and object relatives, based on the frequency of the relatives in the trigger experience and the complexity of the relatives:

$$p(S) = \frac{w_S n_S}{w_S n_S + (1 - w_S) n_{S'}}$$

$$p(O) = \frac{w_O n_O}{w_O n_O + (1 - w_O) n_{O'}}$$

where

$$w_O < w_S < 0.5$$

This means that both object relatives and subject relatives are dispreferred in terms of parsing to non-relativized alternatives (we will come to what those alternatives might be later), and that object relatives are harder to parse than subject relatives. The actual values seem to affect only the rate at which the simulation converges to a stable end point, and the sensitivity of the simulation to initial conditions. The values used for the results shown here were $w_S = 0.4$ and $w_O = 0.3$. The initial speech community was always set to a completely random spread of all four possible language types.

A feature of the simulation results that is immediately striking is the formation of large groups of similar individuals—these appear to be language communities. This is a similar result to one reported by Jules Levin (reported in Keller 1994: 100). Levin's simulation is similar to this one in many respects, but it does not model the influence of selection in parsing or production (transformations T1 and T3 in Figure 2.6). In other words, it assumes that the language that an individual will acquire is simply the one that most of that individual's neighbours has. Keller (1994: 99) calls this 'Humboldt's Maxim':

Talk in a way in which you believe the other would talk if he or she would talk in your place. My thesis is that this maxim—a slightly modified version of Humboldt's own formulation of it—produces homogeneity if the starting point is heterogeneous and stasis if the starting point is homogeneous.

Indeed, this is what happens with Levin's simulation. Starting with a random patterning of two types, the simulation finally settles down with the types clustering together in large groups. (Homogeneity here does not mean complete lack of variety, as there are still two types; rather variation has decreased spatially.)

The result of a typical run of the simulation described here is shown in Figure 3.3. Each small square on the figure is a speaker in the simulation, and the shading for the squares indicates one of the four possible language types. The expected result, if a gradient hierarchy of complexity can explain the accessibility hierarchy, is that the end result should show the types *SO*, *SO'* and *S'O'* (recall that the subject relative universal is ignored for the moment). The only type that should not survive is *S'O*. For clarity, speakers with grammars of this type are indicated by black circles in the diagram. The problem with the results in Figure 3.3 (and with all such runs of the simulation) is that the community converges on only one type: *S'O'*. This clearly poses a serious problem for the complexity hierarchy explanation.

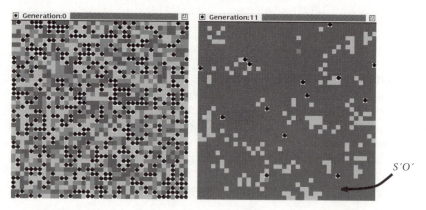

Figure 3.3. The initial and eleventh generations of a simulation run. Each square on the diagrams corresponds to an individual in the arena of use. Each shade of grey corresponds to a language type. The initial distribution of shades is roughly equal between the four types, whereas, in the second diagram, only *S'O'* survives in any significant numbers.

Competing motivations

The solution to this problem involves a 'competing-motivations' explanation (e.g. Givón 1979; DuBois 1987; Hall 1992). These are explanations that rely on functional pressures in *conflict.* Newmeyer (1994*a*) examines several different types of these explanations and argues that *some* attempts by functionalists to build these sorts of motivations directly into their theories of synchronic grammatical phenomena render both their descriptions and their explanations inadequate. These criticisms will not apply to the approach taken in this book, since the functional pressures in question are not assumed to be encoded in grammars. Instead, the I-language domain is taken to be autonomous from the environment;[4] however, as the model described in the previous section makes clear, this does not preclude the possibility that functional pressures can influence the possible states a grammar can take.

Types of complexity

The influence on parsing of structural complexity is *one* functional pressure that affects relative clauses. Because it affects parsing, it is part of what I will call *p-complexity.* The details of a full definition of p-complexity will involve many different aspects, but the influence of it within the selection model is simple:

> **p-complexity.** In comprehension, the selection of competing variants (i.e. variant forms that are synonymous, or functionally undifferentiated) will depend on their relative parsing complexity. So, the more difficult some variant is to parse, the more likely it is to fail to be included in the set of trigger experiences of the child.

Some of the other factors that influence p-complexity are, for example, redundancy of information and configurational markedness (as discussed in Chapter 2). Another type of complexity that will influence the selection model is morphological or *m-complexity*:

> **m-complexity.** In production, the selection of variants will depend on their relative morphological complexity. So, given two competing ways in which to produce some message, the speaker will be more likely to produce the one that is less morphologically complex.

---

[4] However, see Chapter 5 for discussion of a mechanism through which features of the environment *can* become encoded in an autonomous grammar.

Traditional structural markedness, where a marked form has more morphemes (see e.g. Croft 1990: 73, and the discussion in Chapter 2), is clearly related to m-complexity. However, precisely how this affects production is not clear: is the relevant measure the number of morphemes, or the number of morphs? Do all morphemes carry equal m-complexity, or are morphemes that are involved in agreement (ϕ-features) more complex to produce than others (such as definiteness markers)? We shall return to this question later, but, since we will typically be looking at the relative ranking of variants with regard to m-complexity, we need not go further in specifying the details of its definition.

This is a competing-motivations explanation, since it claims that the pressures that these factors bring to bear on the selection of relative clauses are opposed. Consider the following Malagasy examples (from Keenan 1972*b*):

(3.7) ny vehivavy izay nividy ny vary ho an' ny ankizy
     the woman REL bought the rice for   the children
     'the woman who bought the rice for the children'

(3.8) (*a*) *ny vary izay nividy ho an' ny ankizy   ny vehivavy
          the rice REL bought for   the children the woman
          'the rice which the woman bought for the children'

      (*b*) ny vary izay novidin'   ny vehivavy ho an' ny ankizy
          the rice REL bought+PASS the woman for   the children
          'the rice which the woman bought for the children'

(3.9) (*a*) *ny ankizy   izay nividy ny vary (ho an) ny vehivavy
          the children REL bought the rice (for)   the woman
          'the children who the woman bought the rice for'

      (*b*) ny ankizy   izay nividianan'   ny vehivavy ny vary
          the children REL bought+CIRC the woman the rice
          'the children who the woman bought the rice for'

Example 3.7 is an example of a subject relative in Malagasy. Example 3.8*a* shows that object relativization in Malagasy is ungrammatical. This raises the question of how speakers get round the problem of presenting the message in Example 3.8*a* without using the ungrammatical relative. The solution in Malagasy is to promote the object to subject using a passive and then relativizing on the derived subject (Example 3.8*b*). This structure is morphologically marked with respect to the non-passivized equivalent, since it involves extra passive morphology on the verb: hence it has a higher m-complexity. Similarly, Malagasy oblique relatives (Example 3.9*a*) are ungrammatical (as we should expect from the accessibility

Table 3.1. *Initial variables in simulation*

Variable	Values	Interpretation (inverse of)
w_R	$w_R > .5$	m-complexity of RC variants
w_S	$w_S < .5$	p-complexity of subject RC
w_O	$w_O < w_S < .5$	p-complexity of object RC

hierarchy). Instead, speakers can use another promotion-to-subject construction (Example 3.9*b*). Here, a 'circumstantial' affix is attached to the verb that promotes the oblique object to subject. Again, this clearly involves an increase in m-complexity.

Here, then, is a case where avoidance of some relative causes an *increase* in m-complexity, but a *decrease* in p-complexity.[5] Thus, the two complexity motivations are in competition.

Testing the competing motivations

In order to test what effect m-complexity has on the simulation, the way in which I-language is mapped onto utterances (the transformation T1 in Figure 2.6) needs to be adjusted. It is too simplistic to say that speakers produce utterances in line with their I-language states; instead, the probability of producing morphologically simpler forms should be weighted higher than the higher m-complexity variants. To do this, a variable w_R is introduced that represents the speaker preference of *S* and *O* over the higher m-complexity non-relative variants *S'* and *O'*. The parameters of the simulation, therefore, are as shown in Table 3.1.

Depending on the initial conditions, one of two results emerges depending on the relative magnitude of m-complexity and p-complexity. If m-complexity is high, then the end result is languages of type *S'O'* only (as in the previous simulation), whereas, if p-complexity is high, the end result

---

[5] The relative clauses are subject relatives, and thus have smaller structural domains. Hawkins (1994*b*: 31) explicitly states that the calculation of structural complexity should relate to the position of the co-indexed element inside the clause 'in its original (d-structure) position' in an attempt to provide a unified account of promotion-type relatives such as Example 8*b* and non-promoted relatives. However, there are reasons why we should be wary of this approach and, at least as a first approximation, use a definition that refers to the surface position. One of the results of Keenan and Hawkins (1987) work is that, when errors are made repeating relatives, then the errors tend to be towards relatives on higher positions on the hierarchy. The majority of errors made repeating relativized direct objects were relative clauses on the subject of a passive; the majority of errors made repeating relativized subjects of passives, however, were relative clauses on direct objects. A possible explanation is that the former case is a response to p-complexity (the relative clause was mis-parsed), whereas the latter is a response to m-complexity (a simpler paraphrase is produced).

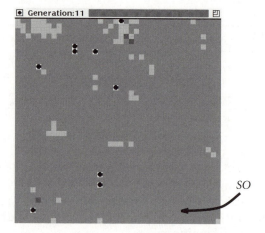

Figure 3.4. The eleventh generation of a simulation run with high p-complexity. In contrast to the previous figure, the arena of use is dominated here by the *SO* type.

is languages of type SO only (see Figure 3.4). Obviously, the required hierarchy fails to emerge in either starting condition.

Although this result seems to suggest that the competing motivations hypothesis has failed, this in fact depends on the values of the variables in Table 3.1. These variables are set to certain values at the start of the simulation and remain the same for all points in the simulation space and over time. However, it is not plausible to say that the relative magnitude of m-complexity and p-complexity will be invariant for languages. To see why, compare the Malagasy examples with some Malay examples, also from Keenan (1972*b*):

(3.10) Ali bunuh ayam   itu dengan pisau
      Ali killed chicken the with   knife
      'Ali killed the chicken with the knife'

(3.11)   (*a*) *pisau yang Ali bunuh ayam   itu dengan
           knife REL Ali killed   chicken the with
           'the knife that Ali killed the chicken with'

       (*b*) pisau yang Ali gunakan untuk membunuh ayam   itu
           knife REL Ali use   for   kill   chicken the
           'the knife that Ali used to kill the chicken'

Malay is unable to relativize on obliques (Examples 3.10–3.11*a*); however, there is no way in which to promote the oblique to subject as in Malagasy

(Example 3.8*b*). When Keenan's informants were asked to produce an equivalent to the English oblique relative, they gave a paraphrase, such as Example 3.11*b*.

As well as paraphrase and promotion, circumlocution is another strategy for avoiding relatives. Consider variants to the English sentences 3.13*a* and 3.12*a*.

(3.12)   (*a*)   I watch the batsman whom England selected.

　　　　(*b*)   I watch the batsman who was selected by England.

(3.13)   (*a*)   I watch the team which Hick plays cricket for.

　　　　(*b*)   *I watch the team which was played cricket for by Hick.

　　　　(*c*)   I watch this team—Hick plays cricket for them.

Example 3.12*b* is the promoted variant of Example 3.12*a*, but the passive is not available to promote the oblique and reduce p-complexity (Example 3.13*b*). Another option in this case is to use something like Example 3.13*c*, which does not have a relative at all.

The point of these examples is to show that the relative m-complexity of relative clauses and their non-relative variants really depends on a variety of factors connected with other systems in the language in question. In certain languages like Malagasy, there is a well-developed voice system that enables promotion to subject. Malay, on the other hand, has a less-well-developed system, and cannot promote obliques. English can promote some noun phrases, but the passive involves higher m-complexity (is morphologically more marked) than the passive in Malagasy. To sum up, the relative magnitude of m- and p-complexity is not universally fixed; rather it is affected by the systems made available by the rest of the language and may vary over time.

To model this, the simulation is adjusted so that every few iterations the relative magnitude of m- and p-complexity is adjusted for a random language type. This involves introducing another parameter that expresses the probability of a change occurring at each iteration, but the value of this parameter does not seem to be too critical. The result of this seemingly small change in the simulation is profound. Instead of settling down to a static end state with only one predominant type like the other simulation runs, the state of the simulation 'world' is constantly changing. Large groups form, as in Levin's simulation, and in my previous simulations, but at the boundaries of these groups something akin to borrowing occurs, and language types move across space, and change prominence over time. A few of the generations in a typical run of the simulation are shown in Figure 3.5. The most important feature of these results is that all language types are well represented *except for S'O*. (This is the type marked as black circles in Figure 3.5.) *S'O* takes up about one quarter of the initial space. By generation 10, however, almost none of the type is displayed. Over a long run, the other three types (indicated for the final generation) share the space roughly between themselves. The implicational universal has emerged.

To summarize, the results from the three simulation experiments are:

1. p-complexity only: static end state—*S'O'*.

2. p- and m-complexity, fixed: static end state—either *S'O'* or *SO*.

3. p- and m-complexity, variable: dynamic state—*S'O'*, *SO'*, and *SO*.

These results lend strong support to a competing-motivations analysis within a selection model where the magnitude of the selection pressures is variable. The next section discusses how this result can be generalized to other positions on the accessibility hierarchy, and gives an explanation for the subject relative universal.

Dynamic typology

In order to understand what the simulation is doing, we need a theory of how dynamic processes give rise to universal constraints. In other words, if we understand what types of changes are likely to occur when the simulation is in one state, then is there a way to calculate what universals will emerge? Borrowing from Greenberg (1978), we will use *type graphs* in order to answer this question.

A type graph is a graph whose nodes are states in a language typology, and whose arcs are possible transitions between those states. So, for the example discussed above, there will be four nodes in the type graph: *S'O'*, *S'O*, *SO'*, and *SO*. As we have seen, possible transitions between these states depend on the relative magnitude of m- and p-complexity. This is represented by two different types of arc: solid ones for when p-complexity considerations are paramount, and dotted ones for when m-complexity outweighs p-complexity (see Figure 3.6).

If we follow the transitions on this graph we can see what happens to a language in the simulation given a particular initial state. So, if a language relativizes on subjects and objects, and the m-complexity of relative-clause variants is low, then the next state of the language will be subject-only

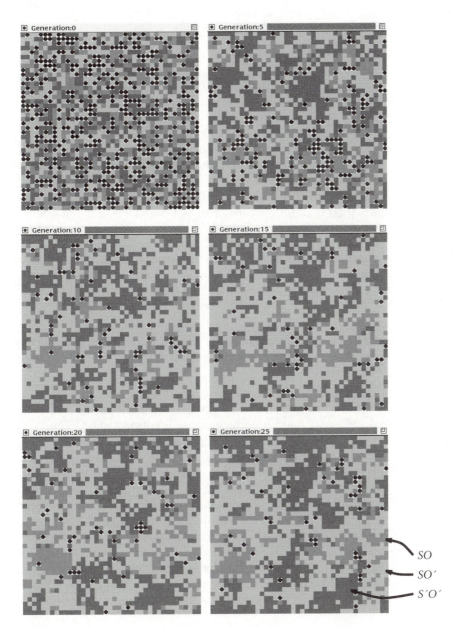

Figure 3.5. An example run of the simulation with shifting complexities. Note that the number of the *S'O* type (here in black) is reduced rapidly from the initial condition. (Proportion of *S'O* is 27% at generation 0, and 3% at generation 25.)

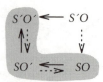

Figure 3.6. A type graph showing the emergence of $O \rightarrow S$.

relativization, and then neither subject nor object relativization.[6] Considering only the solid arcs on the graph, then the situation is equivalent to the first run of the simulation where m-complexity was not considered. It is clear that the inevitable end state will be $S'O'$, since, once a language is in this state, then it cannot escape. This is termed a *sink* by Greenberg (1978: 68). Similarly, if only the dotted arcs are considered, then SO is a sink. This explains why the second simulation run always ended up at one of these two end states depending on the initial conditions.

If both types of arc are considered, then the implicational universal emerges: languages end up in the shaded region of the graph. An informal definition of areas of type graphs that corresponds to universals is given below:

The language types that are predicted to occur are the set of nodes that belong to strongly connected sub-graphs whose members are only connected to other members of the sub-graph.

A node *a* is 'connected' to *b* if there is an arc from *a* to *b*, or if there is an arc from *a* to *c* and *c* is connected to *b*. A graph is 'strongly connected' if for every node *a* and every node *b* in the graph *a* is connected to *b* (and vice versa). So, in Figure 3.6 all the nodes in the shaded region are connected to each other, but once languages are in this region they cannot escape from it.

The graph can be extended to other positions on the hierarchy. So, for example, Figure 3.7 is the graph for the first three positions on the accessibility hierarchy: subject, direct object, and indirect object. Again, the universal that is predicted by the definition above is shaded. The shaded region in Figure 3.7 is indeed what the accessibility hierarchy predicts.

A problem with this result is that it does not correspond to what is found in reality. This is because of the separate subject relative universal which states that all languages relativize on subjects. This is a case where the type-graph theory can be used to look for a possible explanation. The

---

[6] Figure 3.6 shows only what will happen all other things being equal—in other words, if there is sufficient random variation in the environment to allow speakers and hearers to select variant forms freely. The simulation described in the previous section does *not* make this assumption, however, since variation is drawn from other languages which are also following paths through the type graph.

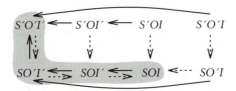

Figure 3.7. A type graph showing how the hierarchy emerges.

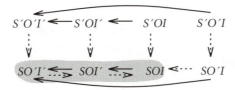

Figure 3.8. The modified type graph including the subject relative universal.

smallest change that can be made to the graph above to bring it in line with the observed universal is to remove the solid arc leading from $SO'I'$ to $S'O'I'$ (i.e. remove the hearer-driven change that makes subject relatives ungrammatical). This is shown in Figure 3.8.

In fact, it seems that this might indeed be the correct modification to the previous explanation. Recall that languages typically provide a number of possible ways of 'avoiding' a particular relative-clause construction. One of the least morphologically complex of these strategies is the promotion-to-subject strategy exemplified by Malagasy (Examples 3.10–3.11). This strategy is *not* available to avoid subject relatives, however, and even if the language allowed demotion this would not be a viable option, since it would increase the p-complexity of the relative clause. So, this calls into question an idealization in the design of the simulation: namely, that relative m- and p-complexity shifts randomly. If promotion is unavailable for subjects, then the average relative m-complexity of constructions that avoid subject relativization will be higher than for other positions. Selection by the speaker—in terms of m-complexity—will thus be more likely for this position.

Case-coding and complexity

So far only *primary* relativization strategies have been considered. These are strategies for relativization that are used for subjects according to Keenan and Comrie's definition. However, languages often make use of different strategies for relativization on lower positions on the hierarchy. It turns out that the competing-motivations approach makes some interesting predictions for the distribution of these strategies.

A strategy taxonomy

Two broad types of relativization strategy are examined in Keenan and Comrie's work on relative clauses:

The case-coding taxonomy.   A strategy for relativization is case-coding (or [+case]) if a nominal element is present in the restricting clause which case marks the relativized noun phrase at least as explicitly as is normally done in simple sentences (adapted from Keenan and Comrie 1977 and Comrie and Keenan 1979).

An example of a [−case] strategy in Arabic relativization is given here (Comrie, personal communication):

(3.14) ar- rajul ya'rifu s-   sayyida allatii naa'ima
        the man knows the woman REL   asleep
        'The man knows the woman who is asleep'

Here the relative marker does not code for the case of the noun phrase in the subordinate clause being relativized, and there is no extra nominal element with the clause that marks its case. Object relativization in Arabic is [+case], however (Comrie, personal communication):

(3.15) al- walad ya'rifu r-   rajul alladhii Darabat -hu s-   sayyida
        the boy   knows the man REL   she:hit   him the woman
        'The boy knows the man whom the woman hit'

In this example, the case is coded by the resumptive pronoun *-hu* within the restrictive clause. Another example of a [+case] strategy is given by standard written English direct-object relativization:

(3.16) The boy knows the man whom we saw.

Here, the relative pronoun marks the relativized noun phrase as a direct object. Notice that the commonly used relative markers (*who, which, that*) occurring in subject and direct-object relativization can all be used for both those positions, and are thus [−case], since they do not explicitly code the case of the relativized noun phrase.

In these examples, and universally, [+case] strategies occur lower on the accessibility hierarchy than [−case] strategies. This is predicted by the theory outlined in this chapter if we include a notion of information content in the definition of p-complexity. When defining the p-complexity of relative clauses it was argued that complexity must be relative to a particular psycholinguistic operation—namely the association of the trace, or resumptive pronoun, with the head noun. The complexity of this association task may be ameliorated by providing (typically redundant) information relating to the grammatical function of the embedded element. Hawkins (1994*a*: 45–6) supports a similar analysis: the 'conservation of logical structure' hypothesis of Keenan (1972*a*). This states that resumptive pronouns make the correspondence between surface structures and logical-semantic structures of relative clauses more transparent, and therefore make processing easier. However, this analysis only covers resumptive pronouns, whereas a treatment in terms of redundancy of information covers the full range of possible [+case] strategies.

The two types of strategy differ with respect to both m- and p-complexity:

[+**case**]: high relative m-complexity (extra nominal element increases morphological markedness), low relative p-complexity.

[−**case**]: low relative m-complexity, high relative p-complexity.

At first sight, this seems to make no predictions about the distribution of strategies. Again, m- and p-complexity are in conflict. However, the relative markedness of the two strategies changes down the accessibility hierarchy:

Change in relative m-complexity. The typical m-complexity of a relative clause high on the hierarchy will be lower than that of one low on the hierarchy, therefore any increase of m-complexity will be more marked the higher it is on the hierarchy.

Change in relative p-complexity. The low positions on the hierarchy have higher p-complexity, so it is less likely that a form that increases p-complexity further will survive to the trigger on these positions.[7]

It is apparent that case-coding represents a trade-off between an increase in m-complexity and a decrease in p-complexity. For positions low on the hierarchy the balance is in favour of selection in terms of p-complexity (hearer selection) giving [+case] strategies, whereas positions high on the

---

[7] Notice that the asymmetry between speaker and hearer selection here is explicable given that speakers make selection 'choices' by comparing the two variants directly, whereas hearers/acquirers do not have direct access to a comparison of the two forms at the point of selection.

hierarchy favour selection in terms of m-complexity (speaker selection) giving [−case] strategies.

Beyond [+/−case]

Tallerman (1990) revises the definition of [+case] to include examples where the relativized noun phrase is marked without an explicit nominal element. The motivation for this is to analyse examples of consonantal mutation in Welsh—which disambiguate the function of the relativized noun phrase—as [+case]. The new definition also includes strategies that explicitly mark the grammatical function of the relativized noun phrase by word order (e.g. English):

> **Case-coding strategies.** A strategy for relativization is case-coding or [+case] if it explicitly signals the grammatical function of the relativized noun phrase, not necessarily with a nominal element (adapted from Tallerman 1990: 293).

In fact, this means that most languages use solely [+case] strategies, in Tallerman's sense, unless word order produces ambiguous relative clauses. Welsh provides examples where there are both [+case] and [−case] strategies, since the basic word order is VSO (Tallerman 1990: 296).

(3.17) y   bachgen a   welodd *t* y   ci   *t*
       the boy   COMP saw-3SG   the dog
       'the boy who saw the dog' or
       'the boy whom the dog saw'

In this example, the *t*s mark the possible positions for the trace, yielding the two possible readings respectively. This is [−case] relativization. As mentioned above, Welsh consonantal mutation provides a [+case] strategy (Tallerman 1990: 300):

(3.18) y   bachgen a   welodd *t* gi
       the boy   COMP saw-3SG   dog(+MUT)
       'the boy who saw a dog'

(3.19) y   bachgen a   welodd ci   *t*
       the boy   COMP saw-3SG dog(−MUT)
       'the boy who a dog saw'

Put simply, there is a morphophonemic set of changes in Welsh known as soft mutation, which occurs on some segments in certain environments, including directly following a noun phrase. Wh-traces are included in the set of triggering environments, hence the mutation of the initial segment in *ci* above.

An interesting feature of Tallerman's definition of [+case] is that it allows us to go beyond the simple case-coding strategies with opposition between speaker and hearer and look in more detail at the interaction of m-complexity and cross-linguistic distribution. First, a further definition:

Zero-morpheme strategy. A strategy that is case-coding (in Tallerman's sense) but uses no extra morphemes ('nominal elements') for case-coding is termed a zero-morpheme strategy.

Hence, Welsh soft mutation is a zero-morpheme strategy. Since zero-morpheme strategies are case-coding, with low relative p-complexity, but *without* the concomitant increase in relative m-complexity, we can predict that zero-morpheme strategies will be used as high up on the accessibility hierarchy as they can be.[8] This is indeed true in the Welsh case. If the so-called word-order strategies in the sample of Maxwell (1979) are taken into account, then this is further support for this prediction, since they are all primary strategies.

We can extend the prediction about zero-morpheme strategies by formulating a hierarchy of strategies that is ranked in terms of m-complexity:

Strategy hierarchy. [+case] strategies may be ordered with respect to the typical relative m-complexity of case-coding, such that a complex or 'weighty' strategy occurs low on the hierarchy:

Zero-morph > Case-coding Relative Pronoun >? Anaphoric Pronoun[9]
(> Clitic Doubling etc.)

The lower the strategy is on this hierarchy, the lower on the accessibility hierarchy that strategy will occur cross-linguistically.

This hierarchy is rather speculative, since there has been no typological research that categorizes strategies to this level of detail. The study of

---

[8] This will generally mean that they will be used for subject relativization (i.e. they will be primary strategies); however, it is conceivable that a zero-morpheme strategy may be constrained in other ways so that it cannot be freely selected for every position on the hierarchy (see also Chapter 4).

[9] The ordering of these two strategies may depend on an assessment of the degree to which the two types of pronoun encode ϕ-features across languages.

Maxwell (1979) refines the Keenan–Comrie sample by categorizing strategies as word order, relative pronoun, and anaphoric pronoun, among others. Maxwell's categorization is obviously not motivated by morphological complexity, and we must be cautious of any support that his work provides. However, it is interesting to note that the distribution of anaphoric-pronoun strategies in the sample is skewed significantly lower on the accessibility hierarchy than that of the relative-pronoun strategies.[10]

Even within one language, we can find support for the strategy hierarchy. Again in Welsh, Tallerman (1990: 313) notes that a pronominal strategy can be used for some direct objects, some non-direct objects, and all genitives. A clitic doubling strategy, however, is only available for some non-direct objects and all genitives. This distribution is expected since the clitic doubling strategy (Example 3.21) has a higher m-complexity than simple retention of an anaphoric pronoun (Example 3.20):

(3.20) y bachgen y   gwnaeth y ci ei   weld
        the boy   COMP did-3SG the dog 3MSG see
        'the boy that the dog saw' (Tallerman 1990: 302)

(3.21) y papur roeddwn   i'n   edrych arno   fo
        the paper COMP-was-1SG I-PROG look   at-3MSG it(3MSG)
        'the paper that I was looking at' (Tallerman 1990: 306)

Extending the explanation

The discussion in this chapter has led to the conclusion that a gradient hierarchy of processing complexity cannot on its own give rise to the cross-linguistic implicational hierarchy of accessibility to relativization. Instead, a shifting competing-motivations explanation is required. This inevitably gives rise to the question: can any implicational universal be explained without competing motivations? The rest of this chapter looks at this question for a few more cases, but any conclusions must be speculative, opening up avenues for future research.

Morphology

The first example relates to a fairly trivial processing/functional explanation in morphology. It should really be considered as a simple illustration of the way in which the method discussed in this chapter can be extended to non-syntactic domains.

---

[10] A Mann-Whitney U test gives us a significance level of $p < 0.005$, but this level may be partially due to the sampling technique.

It is well known (Greenberg 1963) that if a language marks gender distinctions in the first person, then it will mark gender distinctions in the second or third persons or both.

$$\text{For gender marking: } 1 \rightarrow (2 \vee 3)$$

If the competing-motivations approach is as general as the previous sections have suggested, then we can make a direct analogy with the explanation for $O \rightarrow S$ and expect the following sorts of complexity differences:

1. First person gender marking is more complex than second or third person gender marking.
2. The lack of gender marking is in general more complex than gender marking.

On the other hand, the implicational universal above has its *contrapositive* equivalent (see Chapter 1):

$$\text{For no gender marking: } (2 \& 3) \rightarrow 1$$

This means that the other possible complexity differences should be:

1. The lack of second and third person gender marking is more complex than the lack of gender marking on first person.
2. Gender marking is in general more complex than the lack of gender marking.

Only these complexity pressures would give us something like the type graph in Figure 3.6 and hence the implicational universal.

It seems that the latter possibility is the most likely one, especially given that marking gender by definition involves an increase in m-complexity over no gender marking, whatever persons are marked. How can we interpret the competing motivation in this case? Intuitively the hearer must, during parsing, map nominal expressions onto possible referents. The difficulty of this task in part relates to the amount of information about the referent that is encoded in the expression, so gender marking is useful in as much as it aids the mapping of signifier onto signified. It is likely, however, that gender marking is less important for first person expressions since the referent, at least for spoken language, is unambiguously given by context.

It seems then, that p-complexity increases when gender is left unmarked, especially on second and third person expressions, but conversely m-complexity increases when gender is marked on any expression. Again, the relative 'strengths' of these two pressures will vary depending on the structure of the rest of the language as well as with context. So, for example, the difficulty of relating a referent to an expression depends not only on gender marking, but also on the other types of morphological marking made available by the language. This is a direct analogue of the main case described in this chapter, and hence the implicational universal is expected.

Word order revisited

One of the major problems relating to a generalized competing-motivation approach is how it can be combined with the explanation for word-order universals in Chapter 2. In other words, does an explanation based on EIC admit the possibility of other motivations in conflict?

Matrix disambiguation

One of the implicational universals covered by Hawkins (1990, 1994*a*) seems to pose a problem for the EIC approach:

$$VO \rightarrow CompS$$

This means that almost all VO languages are Comp-initial in S′, whereas OV languages are found that are both Comp-initial and Comp-final. EIC leads us to expect the MNCCs of the ICs of the verb phrase to be arranged close together, minimizing the size of the constituent recognition domain. Here the MNCCs of the verb phrase are V and Comp, so the expected optimal orderings are: $_{VP}[V \ _{S'}[Comp \ S]]$ and $_{VP}[_{S'}[S \ Comp] \ V]$, where V and Comp are next to each other. This is also what we would expect from Dryer's (1992) branching direction theory. Both V and Comp are non-branching categories, so in the unmarked case they should order on the same side as their branching counterparts.

What about the other order predicted by the universal: $_{VP}[_{S'}[Comp \ S] \ V]$? This is not a problem for Dryer, since the BDT has nothing to say about *implicational* universals such as these; it refers only to the (parametric) correlations between non-branching categories and verbs, and branching categories and objects—a correlation that is borne out in this case, since CompS is significantly more common amongst VO languages than OV, and SComp is found *only* in OV languages:

there seems to be little question that this is a correlation pair. While both initial and final complementizers are found in OV languages (cf. Dryer 1980; Hawkins 1990: 225), complementizers in VO languages seem invariably to be initial; in fact, it may be an exceptionless universal that final complementizers are found only in OV languages. If so, then final complementizers are clearly more common in OV languages than they are in VO languages, and complementizers are therefore verb patterners, while the Ss they combine with are object patterners.   (Dryer 1992: 101–2)

In other words, the occurrence of OV&CompS is left unexplained.

Hawkins (1994*a*: §5.6.1), on the other hand, suggests that the asymmetry can be explained by looking at the functions of a category like Comp other than mother node construction. Consider the problems that the order $_{VP}[_{S'}[S\ Comp]\ V]$ might cause a hearer. Because the initial category in S′ is S, there is a potential for garden-pathing here; only once the complementizer is reached does the subordinate nature of the preceding clause become apparent (see e.g. Clancy *et al.* 1986 for experimental evidence relating to similar examples involving relative clauses). There is a potential advantage, then, for 'matrix disambiguation' immediately the S′ is encountered.

The following list sets out the parsing preferences of the various language types:

1. VO&CompS: good for EIC, immediate matrix disambiguation.

2. VO&SComp: bad for EIC, non-immediate matrix disambiguation.

3. OV&CompS: bad for EIC, immediate matrix disambiguation.

4. OV&SComp: good for EIC, non-immediate matrix disambiguation.

All the occurring language types either have immediate matrix disambiguation or are good for EIC. Only the non-occurring type is both bad for EIC recognition and does not immediately disambiguate between matrix and subordinate clauses.

This seems to be a neat explanation for the asymmetry. Indeed, it also seems to follow the structure of the explanation for the accessibility hierarchy, in that the two pressures on parsing are in competition for OV languages.[11] One potential problem with it is that there is no definite reason why matrix disambiguation should be singled out as such an important factor in parsing. Why do we not find a preference for immediate genitive disambiguation, for example? Although the matrix/subordinate distinction is particularly significant in language (Hawkins 1994*a*: 325), I believe this weakens the explanation somewhat.

A more crucial problem with this seeming competing motivations explanation can be understood with a type graph, as in Figure 3.9. On this graph, the solid arcs correspond to EIC-motivated changes, and the dotted arcs to changes motivated by immediate matrix disambiguation. It is immediately obvious that this is not the same as Figure 3.6. The shaded area corresponds to the universal predicted by the type-graph theory in this chapter: VO&CompS. This language type is a sink, since there are arcs leading into it, but none leaving it. Essentially, if this language type is the

---

[11] The competition here is not between speaker and hearer, but rather 'within' the hearer. There is nothing in principle in the theory to rule this out, however.

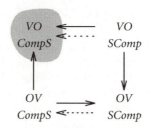

Figure 3.9. A type graph showing problems with the explanation of *VO → CompS.*

best possible for both EIC *and* immediate matrix disambiguation, then why should not all languages end up being that type?

It is not clear what the ultimate solution to this problem might be. One might argue that there are other pressures, as yet unconsidered, in the word-order domain that will mitigate the situation, particularly since EIC shows that the order of all constituents is related if they can appear in the same utterance (i.e. pressures on some other constituent's order may indirectly affect the type graph in Figure 3.9). Alternatively, it may have something to do with the origin of variation. This has so far been considered to be random with respect to the functions being examined (see McGill 1993 for discussion); some of the arcs in the type graph may be 'pruned' if this were not the case.

A different suggestion will be put forward here. So far it has been assumed that selection takes place over utterances. This means that, if an utterance proves hard to parse, then it does not form part of the trigger *and none of the information about word order that it contained will be presented to the LAD.* This seems a sensible stance to take in the absence of decisive experimental evidence about the contents of the trigger experience. On the other hand, an alternative hypothesis might be more realistic. If a structure contains an embedded constituent that is hard to parse, this does not necessarily mean that the branching direction of the superordinate structure cannot be adduced. In the structures being considered here, it may be possible to tell if the verb follows or precedes its object even if the order of Comp and S makes the recognition of the verb phrase difficult. Furthermore, it is likely that there will be more examples of VO order in the rest of the utterances presented to the child that will not involve subordinate clauses. This means that EIC considerations might play their role in the selection of variant orders of Comp and S in S', but not in the selection of variant orders of verb and object, or at least not to the same degree.

If this is the case we can redraw the type graph in Figure 3.9 to include changes between OV and VO which we can assume are random (i.e. not

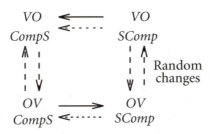

Figure 3.10. A type graph showing what would happen if the verb–object order changed randomly with respect to complementizer order.

affected by the order of S and Comp), as in Figure 3.10. This graph does not, in effect, rule out *any* language types, but the type VO&SComp is predicted to be less common (only one arc leads into it, but three lead out) and this becomes more marked if the languages retain their VO order for longer than the order of their complementizer and subordinate clause (i.e. if the changes in the former are rarer than the latter).

The same approach may also solve a problem with the EIC pointed out in Kirby (1994: 204–6). Wherever there are multiple MNCCs for a particular mother node, there will be a preference for languages that order MNCCs to the left. For example, given that Det and N are both MNCCs for NP, the first MNCC of an NP made up of Det and N in any order will always be the first word in that NP. In both the constructions $_{VP}[V\ _{NP}[Det\ N]]$ or $_{VP}[V\ _{NP}[N\ Det]]$, the CRD will be the optimal two words. (Incidentally, this means that the order of determiner and noun should not be predictable from the order of verb and object. This is indeed the case (Dryer 1992).) For verb-final constructions $_{VP}[_{NP}[Det\ N]\ V]$ or $_{VP}[_{NP}[N\ Det]\ V]$ the CRD cannot be this short, since it will always proceed from the first word of the NP to the verb.

This suggests that head-initial languages will always contain constructions that are easier to parse than their head-final counterparts, and that a type graph of all possible word orders would inevitably lead to a consistently head-initial sink. If, however, selection does not take place at the level of the utterance, and the 'global' frequency of different constructions is taken into account, as suggested above, then it is possible that these small differences will not have this effect.

Of course, this is only a tentative suggestion, the implications of which require testing against historical data and with further simulation work. One fruitful avenue of research would be to look at the influence of parsing on creolization, where we might expect the availability of a huge range of input variation to allow for sampling from the complete range of possible orderings. Hence, the prediction would be that the set of word order types found in creoles is more like the set of ultimately optimal types for principles like EIC.

The prepositional noun-modifier hierarchy

The type-graph approach introduced in this chapter highlights some problems with the explanation for the prepositional noun-modifier hierarchy (repeated below) given in Chapter 2. These problems are far from solved, but once again I will suggest some possible areas where a solution might be found.

In prepositional languages, within the noun phrase, if the noun precedes the adjective, then the noun precedes the genitive. Furthermore, if the noun precedes the genitive, then the noun precedes the relative clause.

For simplicity, let us consider only one of the implicational universals underlying the hierarchy: *GenN* → *AdjN* (for prepositional languages). The explanation given was that genitives were typically longer than adjectives, and in a structure $_{PP}[P_{NP}[Mod\ N]]$ the longer the modifier the worse the corresponding EIC metric. This means, if you like, that there is pressure for a language with prenominal genitives and prenominal adjectives to change its genitive-noun order first. This is backed up by the simulation results in Figure 2.15. This means that the type graph for this universal is as in Figure 3.11. Once again, the problem is clear: the optimal type is a sink, so why do the other types occur? The same thing can be said about the universals *RelN* → *GenN* (Figure 2.16) and *RelN* → *AdjN*. This is the same problem that was faced trying to explain the accessibility hierarchy. In that case the problem was solved by invoking competing motivations, with shifting background conditions. But, in the present case, it is hard to see what competing motivation there could be.

The danger with Figure 3.11 is that it overly simplifies the situation. The mirror-image universal applies for postpositional languages: *NGen* →

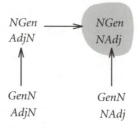

Figure 3.11. A type graph showing that the PrNMH explanation is flawed, since NGen&NAdj is a sink.

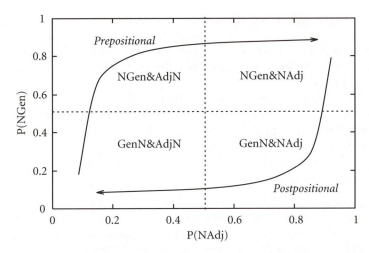

Figure 3.12. The predicted flow of languages through NAdj/NGen space. The top arrow shows the predicted changes for prepositional languages as languages move towards the *NGen&NAdj* sink. The bottom arrow shows how postpositional languages would move back towards the mirror image *GenN&AdjN* sink.

NAdj (for postpositional languages).[12] Although the type graph reveals *NGen&NAdj* to be a sink, this will be true only if language is always prepositional. However, if the order of adposition and noun phrase in a language changes, then the type graph no longer applies, and there will be a new sink (*GenN&AdjN*). This is a case of a markedness reversal. In postpositional languages, the preferred position in EIC terms of the modifier is prenominal. If a speech community is in the sink in Figure 3.11 then such a markedness reversal will tend to start the language moving again (see Figure 3.12).

There are some problems with this suggestion which need further research. For example, if the adpositional order were to change during the transition between the 'harmonic' types AdjN&GenN and NAdj&NGen, then a non-predicted type would arise (i.e. AdjN & NGen & Postp, or NAdj & GenN & Prep). If the rate of adpositional order changes is low enough, then this would not arise; this needs to be tested against historical data. This leaves us with the counter-intuitive position that adposition

---

[12] Interestingly, there is not an equivalent universal *NRel* → *NGen* for postpositional languages. This can be explained in terms of matrix disambiguation, as in the last section. In other words, there is a left–right asymmetry in the order of noun and relative clause, with noun initial being preferred in order to avoid garden-pathing (Clancy *et al.* 1986).

order changes only when it is maximally inefficient for it to do so (e.g. when a prepositional language changes to a postpositional one with consistent NMod order). Again, however, the selection of adpositional order may well be independent of modifier order for the reasons given in the previous section.

These problems aside, I hope that this brief discussion has highlighted the importance of looking carefully at the mechanism linking functional pressures with cross-linguistic universals, before making the assumption that they can be directly correlated.

The agreement hierarchy

The agreement hierarchy of Corbett (1983) is another example of a universal that we might attempt to explain using the principles set out in this chapter. The hierarchy predicts the distribution within and across languages of *syntactic* and *semantic* agreement between a controller and a target. These examples from British English should make the terminology clearer:

(3.22) (*a*) This team played cricket.

(*b*) *These team played cricket.

(3.23) (*a*) The team plays cricket.

(*b*) The team play cricket.

(3.24) (*a*) ?The team won the game it played.

(*b*) The team won the game they played.

Examples 3.22*a* and 3.22*b* show that *team* is syntactically singular. *Team* is the controller here, and the attributive modifier *this* agrees with it syntactically. In Example 3.23*a* the predicate *plays* also agrees with the controller syntactically. Example 3.23*b* is an example of another possibility: 'semantic' plural agreement. This option is also available for the anaphoric pronoun in Example 3.24*b*. In fact, some speakers find Example 3.24*b* better than Example 3.24*a*, where there is syntactic agreement between the controller and the anaphoric pronoun target.

Corbett (1983) looks at syntactic and semantic agreement in Slavic languages in some detail, and proposes the agreement hierarchy:

attributive modifier > predicate > relative pronoun > personal pronoun

For any controller that permits alternative agreement forms, as we move rightwards along the Agreement Hierarchy, the likelihood of semantic agreement will increase monotonically. In absolute terms, if semantic agreement is possible in a given position in the hierarchy it will also be possible in all the positions to the right. In relative terms, if alternative agreement forms are available in two positions, the likelihood of semantic agreement will be as great or greater in the position to the right than in that to the left.   (Corbett 1983: 10–11)

The English examples above correspond to three positions on the hierarchy: attributive modifier, predicate, and personal pronoun. Many cases in Slavic languages are given by Corbett as evidence for the hierarchy, including ones in which the relative pronoun agrees with its controller.

For example, the Czech noun *děvče* 'girl' is syntactically neuter singular. Semantic feminine agreement is possible with personal pronouns (Example 3.27) (data from Vanek 1977, cited in Corbett 1983: 11–12):

(3.25) to   děvče se vdalo
        that(neut) girl   got married(neut)

(3.26) najmula jsem děvče, které   přišlo včera
        hired   did girl   which(neut) came yesterday
        'I hired the girl who came yesterday.'

(3.27) to děvče přišlo včera,   ale já jsem je   /ji   nenajmula
        that girl came yesterday but I did   it(neut)/her(fem) not hire

Another example involves the Russian noun *vrač*, which is syntactically masculine, but can enter into semantically feminine agreement relations when referring to a woman. This is true generally for Russian nouns which refer to people belonging to certain professions (data from Panov 1968, cited in Corbett 1983: 31–2):

(3.28) (*a*) Ivanova— xorošij   vrač
               Ivanova (is) a good(masc) doctor

        (*b*) Ivanova— xorašaja   vrač
               Ivanova (is) a good(fem) doctor

(3.29) (*a*) vrač   prišel
               the doctor came(masc)

        (*b*) vrač   prišla
               the doctor came(fem)

The percentage of informants selecting feminine agreement in a questionnaire study was higher for the predicate targets (Examples 3.29*a*–3.29*b*) than for the attributive targets (Examples 3.28*a*–3.28*b*).

I propose that an explanation for this hierarchy can take exactly the same form as that proposed for the accessibility hierarchy. First, we need a definition for the syntactic complexity of the agreement relations in the above examples:

Structural complexity of agreement.   The structural complexity is calculated by counting the nodes in the *agreement domain*.

Agreement domain.   The agreement domain consists of that subset of nodes dominated by the lowest node dominating both target and controller that structurally integrate the target.

Structural integration of a node X in C.   The set of nodes which structurally integrate X in C are:

- all nodes dominating X within C (including C itself);
- all or some sisters of X (depending on surface coding conventions);
- all sisters of the nodes dominating X within C.

This is an exact parallel of the definition of relativization domains, except that the node C differs depending on the target (i.e. for attributive modifiers C will be D′, for relative pronouns DP, and for predicates and many personal pronouns the node C will be IP). This is to be expected, since structural complexity is a general measure of tree-complexity relative to some psycholinguistic operation. Here, the assumption is that *syntactic* agreement involves some unique psycholinguistic operation.

The tree structures for Examples 3.22–3.24 are shown in Figures 3.13–3.15, with the agreement domains circled. This shows a clear increase in the structural complexity of agreement for the different targets. More generally, the structural templates in Table 3.2 show that the positions of the agreement hierarchy correspond to a hierarchy of structural complexity (where an *a* subscript indicates agreement).

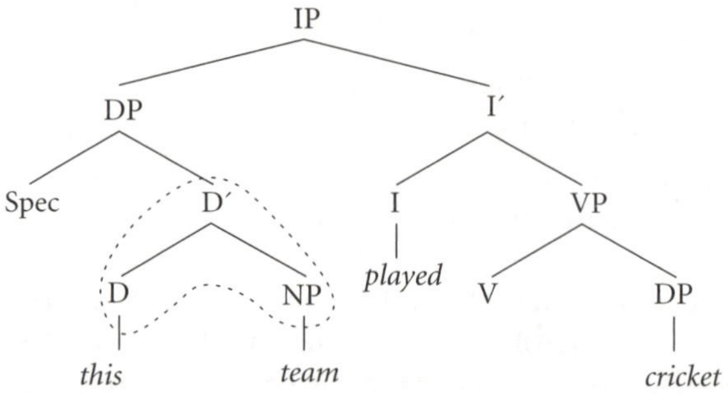

Figure 3.13. The tree structure for attributive agreement.

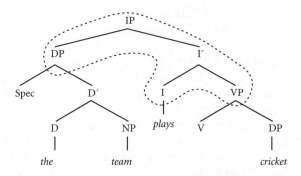

Figure 3.14. The tree structure for predicate agreement.

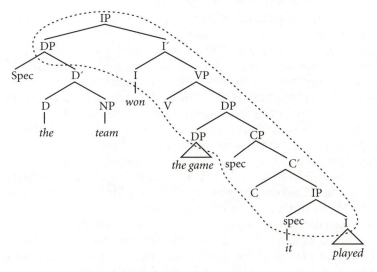

Figure 3.15. The tree structure for personal pronoun agreement.

Table 3.2. *Varieties of agreement*

Agreement type	Structure
Attributive	$_{DP}\{N_a \ldots Mod_a\}$
Predicate	$_{IP}\{_{DP}\{N_a \ldots\} \ _{Pred}\{V/Adj_a \ldots\}\}$
Relative pronoun	$_{DP}\{N_a \ldots _{CP}\{wh_i \ _{IP}\{t_{i/a} \ldots\}\}\}$
Anaphoric pronoun	$\{N_a \ldots Pron_a\}$

These structural templates are intended to show that the range of possible structures that could be involved for each target involves an increasing syntactic 'distance' in terms of agreement domains. The domain for the attributive modifier will typically involve only the sisters of N. The domain for the predicate will include all the nodes dominating the predicate within S, their sisters and the nodes dominating N in the noun phrase. The domain for relative pronoun fits into the hierarchy in this place only on the assumption that its trace carries agreement features in some way, extending the agreement domain arbitrarily deep within the clause. In this view, the target is not the relative pronoun itself, but the whole chain including the wh-element and the co-indexed trace. The potential domain for anaphoric pronouns is the largest, since the target and controller can be in different matrix clauses.

Now that a tentative definition of the structural complexity of agreement has been defined, we are left with exactly the same problems as with the accessibility hierarchy earlier in this chapter. It is not good enough simply to define a structural complexity hierarchy and assume it directly gives rise to a cross-linguistic hierarchy, because one needs to explain why not all languages opt for minimum complexity—that is, the top end of the hierarchy. The competing motivation in this case is probably something to do with the role of agreement in parsing (Hawkins 1994a: 366–73). Essentially, syntactic ϕ-features can act as extra (redundant) information about the structure of the parse. In Hawkins's terms, they can increase the construction potential of a node in parsing. Exactly how this interacts with the principles underlying EIC needs some working out, but the basic point is clear: syntactic agreement gives the hearer information at one point in the parse about other nodes in the parse.

In summary, syntactic agreement has a cost associated with structural complexity of agreement domains, and this complexity increases along the agreement hierarchy. In conflict with this is a parsing preference for redundancy of information that is provided by syntactic agreement. Just as similar competing motivations cause the accessibility hierarchy to emerge, the agreement hierarchy should emerge with these pressures in place. Clearly, there are many details of this putative explanation that need to be worked through. For example, does the definition of agreement domains make the correct performance predictions? Is the preference for small agreement domains a speaker- or hearer-driven pressure? These questions and others that arise from the specific approach to implicational universals expounded in this chapter will have to wait for future research.

Instead, the next chapter turns to cases where the general functional approach appears to fail and asks the question: what are the limits of adaptation?

4   The Limits of Functional Adaptation

In the previous two chapters I have argued that various universals, both parametric and hierarchical can be explained by examining the way in which processing complexity affects the transmission of language through the arena of use.[1] Computer simulations of language as a complex adaptive system have been useful in demonstrating the validity of this approach, as well as highlighting the limitations of previous explanations for hierarchies. The overall goal has been to solve the problem of linkage by enriching the structure of the arena of use proposed by Hurford (1990).

Now that a workable solution for the problem of linkage has been put forward, and given the stipulation that shifting competing motivations are required to explain hierarchical universals, it might be tempting to return to the situation outlined in the first chapter and accept any explanation that equates processing complexity and cross-linguistic distribution. Specifically, can we not now expect a cross-linguistic asymmetry whenever there is a psycholinguistic asymmetry?

This chapter looks at this question and answers it in the negative. It discusses some examples where a processing asymmetry does not give rise to a cross-linguistic asymmetry, and others where linguistic asymmetries appear to be related to the 'wrong' processing asymmetries. These results, then, appear to be fatal to the selection approach and, arguably, functional approaches in general. However, understanding these anomalies properly involves a radical reassessment of the role of innateness in explanation, and offers an interesting challenge to those trying to uncover the nature of universal grammar.

Another selection pressure on relative clauses

In the discussion on the accessibility of noun phrases to relativization in the previous chapter, relative clauses were categorized according to the grammatical function of the trace, or resumptive pronoun, within the subordinate clause. So, for example, the following sentences exemplify the first two positions on the hierarchy:

(4.1) The man who found me saw Ruth (subject)

(4.2) The man whom I found saw Ruth (object)

---

[1] A shorter version of parts of this chapter appears as Kirby (1998b).

Any such categorization is based on choices about what is relevant to typology, and what is not. It could be argued that a categorization on the basis of the number of phonemes in the subordinate clause is equally valid, for example. It is unlikely that this would illuminate any particularly interesting cross-linguistic facts, however. In this section, the categorization of relative clauses will be enriched by taking into account the grammatical function of the head noun in the matrix clause. This is also an available option and, as will be seen, it is commonly discussed in the psycholinguistic literature.

If our attention is restricted solely to the grammatical functions subject and object the following four categories of relative clause are distinguished:

(4.3) The man who found me saw Ruth (matrix subject, subject relative)

(4.4) The man whom I found saw Ruth (matrix subject, object relative)

(4.5) Ruth saw the man who found me (matrix object, subject relative)

(4.6) Ruth saw the man whom I found (matrix object, object relative)

A notation of the form X^Y will be used to signify a relative clause whose head noun has the function X in the matrix clause and whose trace, or resumptive pronoun, has the function Y in the subordinate clause.[2] The four sentences above are examples of S^S, S^O, O^S, and O^O respectively.

One selection pressure on these relative clause types has been reviewed already. A study by Keenan and Hawkins (1987) looks at how native English speakers' ability to repeat relative clauses is dependent on the function of the trace in the subordinate clause. In their work Keenan and Hawkins make no mention of matrix function, so we can characterize their results as follows on the assumption that their results should be generalizable to all relative clauses:

$$\{S^S, O^S\} > \{S^O, O^O\} \quad \text{(accessibility)}$$

The first experiments on the role of matrix function *and* subordinate function were carried out by Sheldon (1974). She used an enactment task with English-speaking children and showed that relative clauses were easier to process if the matrix function of the head matched the function of the trace in the subordinate clause. The results of this study, then, are:

$$\{S^S, O^O\} > \{O^S, S^O\} \quad \text{(parallel function)}$$

[2] The notation used in the literature is simply XY. This is avoided since, in the previous chapter, language types were signified using a similar notation. So, for example, SO signified a language type allowing both subject and object relatives. S^O, on the other hand, means a relative clause such as *the man whom I found saw Ruth.*

This result has proven hard to replicate (MacWhinney and Pleh 1988) and many studies have been carried out that give other rankings of structures in English. For example, DeVilliers *et al.* (1979) gives the results $\{S^S, O^S\} > O^O > S^O$ with a similar enactment task. Clancy *et al.* (1986: 252) summarize the results of Sheldon (1974) and Tavakolian (1981) for their 5-year-old subjects as giving evidence for $S^S > O^O > O^S > S^O$, which is in accord with their own study of Korean.

MacWhinney (1982) and MacWhinney and Pleh (1988) review nine different enactment studies and note that 'the results show remarkable consistency for the pattern $S^S > \{O^S, O^O\} > S^O$' (MacWhinney and Pleh 1988: 117). They also cite studies of French and German (Grimm *et al.* 1975; Kail 1975; Sheldon 1977) that lend support to this ranking. Their own study of Hungarian also bolsters this ranking, at least for unmarked word orders.

Clearly, this is a controversial area, and many different factors have been proposed to account for the rankings. However, the results given above, although appearing to be in conflict, are not inconsistent with an interaction of both parallel function and accessibility. To see this, consider the two possible combinations of these factors. Either accessibility will be a more important factor than parallel function or vice versa:

$$S^S > O^S > O^O > S^O \quad \text{(accessibility > parallel function)}$$
$$S^S > O^O > O^S > S^O \quad \text{(parallel function > accessibility)}$$

All the rankings discussed so far are compatible with one of these possibilities (in other words, there are no predicted differences in any of the results that are not also predicted by one of the two rankings above). It is quite possible that *both* of these rankings are correct, and other factors relating to particular experimental materials such as the sentences under investigation mean that either accessibility or parallel function becomes the more important factor. If this is the case then over all possible relative clauses the ranking would be:

$$S^S > \{O^S, O^O\} > S^O \quad \text{(accessibility} = \text{parallel function)}$$

This is the same as the ranking of MacWhinney and Pleh (1988), although they do not argue for a combined accessibility–parallel function account of their results.

Before continuing, it should be pointed out that these two processing asymmetries have a different theoretical status. Accessibility has been given support by Hawkins's independent complexity theory, as discussed in the previous chapter, whereas parallel function (or any other possible determinant of processing difficulty) is not supported in this way. This might suggest that accessibility is after all the only factor influencing relative-clause complexity. The problem with this is that it fails on its own to predict (although it is consistent with) the psycholinguistic results, particularly the result on which there is least disagreement—that S^O relatives are harder to process than any others. It is not easy to work out what other universal principles are in operation, but clearly there is something more than accessibility at work. Let us assume for the moment that parallel function acts as a selection pressure in the arena of use.

A failure of the functional approach

In the previous chapter a competing-motivations explanation for the accessibility hierarchy was put forward that related the processing asymmetry $S > O$ with the cross-linguistic asymmetry $O \rightarrow S$, given a competing dispreference for non-relativized alternatives. In the notation given above this means that $\{S^S, O^S\} > \{S^O, O^O\}$ gives rise to $(O^O \vee S^O) \rightarrow (S^S \vee O^S)$. In order to test any such predicted universal, we can rewrite the implication as $(S^S \vee O^S) \& \neg (O^O \vee S^O)$. The language types that we expect to find if accessibility influences the selection of relative clauses are therefore:

(a) $S^S \& \neg O^O$

(b) $S^S \& \neg S^O$

(c) $O^S \& \neg O^O$

(d) $O^S \& \neg S^O$

As discussed in the previous chapter, Keenan and Comrie's (1977) accessibility hierarchy explicitly states that all these language types exist:

For each position on the AH, there are possible languages which can relativize that position with a primary strategy, but cannot relativize any lower positions with that strategy.   (Comrie and Keenan 1979: 653)

In principle there is no reason why any other asymmetrical pressure on the processing of relative clauses should not also give rise to an implicational universal. In other words, there is nothing in the logic of the competing-motivations explanation that rules out parallel function as a further factor in determining the p-complexity of RCs. Following the same logic as above, the influence of parallel function $\{S^S, O^O\} > \{O^S, S^O\}$ should give rise to the universal $(O^S \vee S^O) \rightarrow (S^S \vee O^O)$. This can be rewritten as a conjunction: $(S^S \vee O^O) \& \neg (O^S \vee S^O)$. Evidence for parallel function cross-linguistically should come as the following language types:

(*a*) $S^S \& \neg O^S$

(*b*) $S^S \& \neg S^O$

(*c*) $O^O \& \neg O^S$

(*d*) $O^O \& \neg S^O$

The second type corresponds to the second type giving evidence for accessibility and turns up as Iban, for example. The first, third, and fourth types have not been found (although see the following section for apparent counter-evidence).

There is, therefore, no currently available evidence for parallel function showing up cross-linguistically (although proving that some language type does not exist is impossible). Perhaps the problem is that the processing pressures are being considered in isolation, whereas we have argued that a combination of accessibility and parallel function is acting on the processing of relative clauses. The complexity hierarchy $S^S > \{O^S, O^O\} > S^O$ should give rise to the implicational universals:

$$S^O \rightarrow (O^S \vee O^O)$$
$$S^O \rightarrow S^S$$
$$(O^S \vee O^O) \rightarrow S^S$$

In turn these can be rewritten as conjunctions:

$$(O^S \vee O^O) \& \neg S^O$$
$$S^S \& \neg S^O$$
$$S^S \& \neg(O^S \vee O^O)$$

The predicted types are therefore:

(*a*) $O^S \& \neg S^O$

(*b*) $O^O \& \neg S^O$

(*c*) $S^S \& \neg S^O$

(*d*) $S^S \& \neg O^S$

(*e*) $S^S \& \neg O^O$

Once again, some of these types do occur (1, 3, and 5), but these are simply the ones that we have evidence for from the work on the accessibility hierarchy. The critical types regarding the added influence of parallel function are 2 and 4, and there is currently no evidence for the existence of these language types.

In summary, if parallel function has the same status as accessibility in terms of its influence on the functional adaptation of languages within the selection model (and there is no a-priori reason why it should not), then we should find:

(*a*) languages that allow subject relative clauses *unless they are in object position in the matrix*, or

(*b*) languages that allow object relative clauses *unless they are in subject position in the matrix.*

Unfortunately, neither of these language types seems to exist.

This poses serious problems for the functional approach put forward in this book so far. There is nothing in the theory that can explain why accessibility has cross-linguistic implications, but parallel function has not. It seems that the explanations put forward here suffer from being *ad hoc*, a common criticism of functional explanations (see e.g. Lass 1980).

Innate constraints on adaptation

The failure of parallel function to show up cross-linguistically seems to be a fatal blow for functional explanations, but this is because we have so far been looking at only one side of the coin as regards the adaptive nature of language. The map of transformations in the cycle of acquisition and use from Chapter 2 is shown again in Figure 4.1. So far, we have only been concerned with the transformations T1 and T3 (production and parsing), treating the relationship between trigger and competence (T4) as a simple mapping. Recall that the simulations in the previous two chapters treated competence as a list of utterance types—individual grammars were 'acquired' by compiling such a list directly from the trigger experience. The only assumption that was made was that acquisition is an all-or-nothing process. In other words, the acquired competence does not directly reflect subtle frequency effects in the trigger (although marked variants can be acquired as marked variants having something like 'foreign language status'). This is clearly a gross simplification of what is actually going on in acquisition, but it is justified in as much as we believe that the function-mapping trigger onto competence does not affect the viability of variants over time. Furthermore, though less obviously, it also rests on an assumption that the medium of representation of competence does not also affect variant viability.

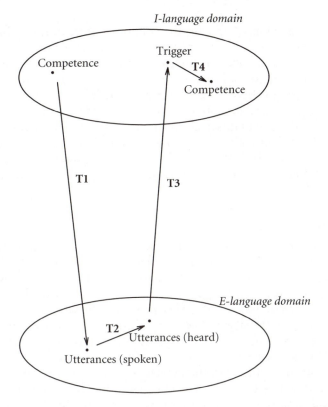

Figure 4.1. Transformations within and between *I-* and *E-domains.*

It is quite possible that something about the process of acquisition distorts the distribution of variants in the trigger in more profound ways than assumed so far. This might be due to constraints imposed by the acquisition device, or it might be due to constraints imposed by the nature of competence itself. In other words, the mental representation system that underlies I-language may not in fact be able accurately to represent features of the trigger experience. If this were true, then certain *constraints on adaptation* should be expected.

Constraints on adaptation in biology

Before going on to explore the implications of constraints imposed by acquisition or competence, it might be useful to look at a similar problem that crops up in another field of complex adaptive systems.

As was discussed in Chapter 1, the adaptive nature of forms in the biological world has much in common with the adaptive nature of language. Both exhibit, to some extent, a striking 'fit' of form to function which inevitably leads us to look for an explanation of that form in terms of function. Although there are a number of crucial differences, the theory that links function and form in language proposed here has much in common with neo-Darwinian selection theory. Indeed, both areas have their generalized form in a theory of complex adaptive systems (Gell-Mann 1992: §2.2.3). It will be instructive, therefore, to look at a couple of cases of mismatches between form and function in biological evolution discussed by Gould (1983: 147–65).

The non-occurrence of a form

Imagine you are an engineer attempting to design some mechanism for moving a machine efficiently over a flat surface. A good design would maximize the distance-to-work ratio of the machine. Given enough time, it is likely that you would plump for a design that has been used by engineers time and time again to solve this very problem: the wheel.

Wheels are functional because they minimize friction when a body is moving over ground, and they stay with the body as it moves (unlike rollers). Although wheels are not as versatile as legs, for example, in terms of the terrain they can cross, the bicycle is a good example of the combination of the two that is amazingly effective at increasing the mobility and speed of a human being. Given that wheels are so functional—they are perfect examples of 'fit' between form and function—it is surprising that they are vanishingly rare in the biological world. Human beings are the only organisms with wheels, and even for us they are part not of our biological phenotype, but of our 'extended phenotype' in Dawkins's (1982) terms. In other words, we do not grow wheels, but have to fashion them from raw materials in our surroundings. Here then is an apparent failure of the theory of natural selection. The forms that occur across the biological kingdom do not live up to expectations; there is a mismatch between form and function.

The solution to this problem lies in the nature of wheels:

a true wheel must spin freely without physical fusion to the solid object it drives. If wheel and object are physically linked, then the wheel cannot turn freely for very long and must rotate back, lest connecting elements be ruptured by the accumulated stress.   (Gould 1983: 160)

The problem for biological organisms is that the parts that make up the organism must be physically connected in order for nutrients to flow between them. As Gould points out, some of our bones are disconnected, but require a surrounding envelope of tissues preventing their free, or wheel-like, rotation.[3] It is impossible, then, for biological wheels (as opposed to wheels made of non-living matter) to exist in the physical world because of a constraint on permissible forms.

Wheels work well, but animals are debarred from building them by structural constraints inherited as an evolutionary legacy. Adaptation does not follow the blueprints of a perfect engineer. It must work with parts available.   (Gould 1983: 164)

The occurrence of a non-functional form

As well as the possibility of an expected form not turning up in biology, Gould gives an example of an unexpected form that cannot be understood without looking at constraints on adaptation. The particular example may initially seem irrelevant to work on language universals; however, as we shall see, the similarities between this and the case of parallel function in relative clauses is striking.

The external genitalia of the female spotted hyena are remarkably similar to those of the male of species (so much so, that medieval bestiaries commonly assumed that the hyena was androgynous). This unusual similarity begs an explanation, although the selective advantage to the female of appearing to be male is rather hard to understand. One attempt at an explanation suggests that the female genitalia evolved for use in a meeting ceremony, where typically more conspicuous structures would have an advantage in 'getting the owner recognized'. However, Gould points out:

Speculation about adaptive significance is a favourite . . . ploy among evolutionary biologists. But the question 'What is it for?' often diverts attention from the more mundane but often more enlightening issue, 'How is it built?'   (Gould 1983: 152)

Gould's argument runs that male and female hyena genitalia are similar because the embryological development of the structures follows the same course. In the genetically coded programme for ontogenetic growth there is nothing that forces the female and male structures to differentiate.[4] The point is that we do not have to explain the existence of the occurrence of the female form—it is forced on the hyena by constraints on the pathways of embryological development.

---

[3] It turns out that there is an exception to this rule. *Escherichia coli* has flagella that act like propellers. They are able to escape the constraint on physical connection only because of their small size. Nutrients and impulses are conveyed between the separate parts by diffusion.

[4] Of course, it is not impossible for other similar organisms to have this differentiation coded in the genome (such as other species of hyena); however, this entails reducing levels of hormones in the female of the species. Gould suggests that the high levels of the hormones in the female spotted hyena are adaptive in some other way.

Formal constraints on relative clauses

The examples from biology show that the adaptation of forms to fit some function can be limited by physical constraints on morphogenesis. This can mean that an expected form does not show up, and, more unexpectedly, that non-functional forms can exist. This means, as Gould argues forcefully, that it is not possible simply to equate function with form. Mismatches are the expected outcome of the system into which adaptive changes must be born.

For the hyena, the external sexual characteristics of the female are forced upon her by physical constraints on embryological development; they are a side effect, if you like, of the existence of similar structures in the male of the species. Can a similar argument be used to explain why it is not possible to get a parallel-function relative clause without also getting the non-parallel-function equivalent? If so, the absence of the expected cross-linguistic asymmetry should not cause us to reject the functional approach.

There must be something about the transformation from trigger experience to competence (the transformation mediated by the LAD) that forces the language user to acquire O^S relatives whenever S^S relatives are acquired, and S^O relatives whenever O^O relatives are acquired. The tree in Figure 4.2 is the familiar formal representation of a relative clause. Although the details of this representation may vary slightly from one syntactic theory to another, the important characteristics for this argument are uncontroversial.

First, notice that the trace dominated by IP, the wh-element in Spec, and the nominal head in DP are all related in some way. The interpretation of a relative clause such as *the man whom I found* requires this. The relative pronoun *who* is related to the trace position (as can be seen by the *who/whom* distinction in certain registers of English); this is indicated by co-indexation. Furthermore, the head of the relative clause, *the man*, must be interpreted as being the logical object of the subordinate construction. The operator *who* in the relative clause is a referential expression standing in for the head noun, and sharing its ϕ-features. So, in many languages the relative pronoun agrees in person, number, and gender with the head. This relation is also shown by co-indexation; in Principles and Parameters theory, the relationship between the head noun and the relative pronoun is actually assumed to be between the head noun and the 'chain' of wh-element and trace. Hence, all three are co-indexed.

The formal mechanisms by which these elements are related might vary from theory to theory. A standard assumption is that the wh-element has moved from the position of the trace in the subordinate clause. The head DP is in a 'predication relation' with the CP, which inherits the trace of the wh-element in specifier position by some kind of generalized Spec-head agreement. Whatever the theory, there are two distinct operations going on: one relating trace and relative pronoun, and the other relating the head noun with the subordinate clause. It is unlikely that these two operations, predication and wh-movement, could be subsumed under one mechanism in any grammatical formalism.

Now, in general, there may be constraints on the operation of mechanisms such as predication and wh-movement. These may be universal in nature or language specific, forming part of the native-speaker competence for the language. If parallel function were to be realized cross-linguistically, the language types $O^O \& \neg S^O$ or $S^S \& \neg O^S$ should show up. If such a language were to exist, it would fall to language-specific constraints on the operation of predication and wh-movement to express the grammaticality of the parallel-function relatives and the ungrammaticality of the non-parallel-function variants. However, in order to express exactly these grammaticality facts, any constraint on predication would need to be dependent on information about wh-movement, or vice versa.

However, it is generally assumed that an operation like predication cannot be sensitive to the internal structure of the CP, and similarly wh-movement cannot be restricted on the basis of structure outside the CP. The two operations in this structure are informationally encapsulated from one another. This means that, if these grammatical facts are mirrored in the LAD, the predicted language types are actually impossible to acquire

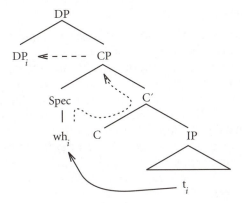

Figure 4.2. The structure of an abstract relative clause. The wh-word is generated internally to the subordinate clause and moves up to the specifier postion. The subordinate clause is adjoined to the maximal DP, which contains the head nominal. The expression in DP$_i$ is co-indexed with the trace via wh-movement, Spec-head agreement, and predication.

or represent in the I-language domain of Figure 4.1. If a child acquires competence in response to a parallel-function relative, then she cannot help but also acquire competence for the non-parallel equivalent. If the non-parallel-function form is made ungrammatical, then the parallel-function variant goes too.

The transformation T3 will tend to filter out the forms that are more complex to process. So, the theory of linguistic selection predicts that the proportion of, say, S^O variants relative to O^O variants that form part of the trigger should be lower than the proportion in the language data. However, given this differential distribution, the LAD (transformation T4) can do only one of two things: both variants can be made ungrammatical, or both variants can be made grammatical (Figure 4.3). Even if *no* S^O variants made it into the trigger, they could still be acquired by the child.

A possible counter-example to the constraint on adaptation

The argument put forward in the previous section seems to explain why the functional explanation for the accessibility hierarchy does not generalize to other processing asymmetries in relative-clause constructions. The whole approach is put into jeopardy, however, if there are any counter-examples to the encapsulation of principles outlined above. This section introduces a case where a language appears to have responded at least partially to pressures from parallel function.

German free relatives

The apparent counter-example comes from a sub-type of German relative-clause constructions. The constructions in question are free, or headless, relatives—relative clauses lacking a head noun (see e.g. Groos and van Riemsdijk 1979). Given that these constructions are rather different from the standard headed, restrictive relatives that we have been considering so far, it is not at all clear that the psycholinguistic results about relative processing complexity should apply. However, if these constructions exhibit a grammaticality constraint that involves the interaction of matrix function and subordinate function, then the argument put forward in the previous section about an innate limitation on the format of constraints will be put in doubt.

In fact, German free relatives (at least for some native speakers) do exhibit just this kind of grammaticality pattern (Cann and Tait 1990: 25):

(4.7)   (*a*) Ich muss wen   du mir empfiehlst nehmen
              I   must who(acc) you to   me   recommend take
              'I must take who you recommend to me'

(*b*) *Ich muss wer   einen guten Eindruck   macht nehmen
     I   must who(nom) a   good impression makes take
     'I must take whoever makes a good impression'

(*c*) *Ich muss wem   du   vertraust nehmen
     I   must who(dat) you trust   take
     'I must take whoever you trust'

Example 4.7*a* is an example of an O^O free relative, whereas Example 4.7*b* is an example of an O^S relative, and is ungrammatical. There is not a simple constraint allowing O^O and not O^S, however, since Example 4.7*c* is an O^O relative, but is also ungrammatical.

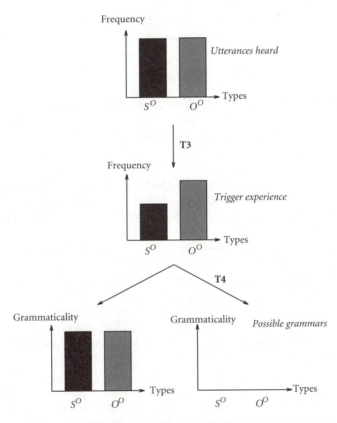

Figure 4.3. The possible pathways of S^O and O^O variants. Even though the relative frequency of S^O may be reduced through selection by the processor, this cannot be reflected in patterns of grammaticality.

The pattern of grammaticality is predicted by comparing the morphological case of the relative pronoun, and the case assigned by the matrix verb. In Example 4.7*a* the accusative relative pronoun matches the accusative case assigned by *nehmen*, but in the other examples there is a 'clash' between the case assigned by the verb and the morphological case of the relative pronoun. This does not explain what is going on in German, however, because the equivalent headed relatives are all grammatical:

(4.8)   (*a*) Ich muss den Mann den   du mir   empfiehlst nehmen
           I   must the man   who(acc) you to me recommend take
           'I must take the man who you recommend to me'

      (*b*) Ich muss den Mann der   einen guten Eindruck   macht nehmen
           I   must the man   who(nom) a   good impression makes take
           'I must take the man who makes a good impression'

      (*c*) Ich muss den Mann dem   du vertraust nehmen
           I   must the man   who(dat) you trust   take
           'I must take the man who you trust'

Example 4.7*a–c*, then, seems to allow some way for information about the grammatical function of the trace to interact with information about the grammatical function of the complex noun phrase. This will be a problem for the theory if these free relatives are assigned a structure similar to that in Figure 4.2.

Can and Tait's (1990) analysis of these constructions suggests that this is not the case. The tree in Figure 4.4 has the subordinate clause generated internally to the noun phrase, rather than adjoined to the DP. In this structure, the DP dominating the relative pronoun *wen* has moved from within the IP up to the specifier of CP as normal. This forms a chain (DP_i, t_i), which is assigned accusative case by *empfiehlst*. A further movement of *wen* to the head of the maximal DP is forced in the theory proposed by Cann and Tait. This movement is required to satisfy a phonetic form licensing principle that has the effect of restricting the occurrence of phonetically null nodes that do not form a part of a chain headed by a licensed node; in this case, the head of the DP is dominated by CP, the noun, and the head of the maximal DP.[5] Given this obligatory movement, the maximal DP inherits the case carried by its head *wen*. The category DP cannot be

---

[5] This is not the place to discuss the details of Cann and Tait's phonetic-form licensing principle (PFLP); suffice to say that it is motivated by the need to constrain the set of functional projections that the language acquirer has to postulate by requiring every syntactic projection to have some phonological representation. It is interesting to note that this principle is very similar to Hawkins's (1994*a*) axiom of MNCC existence, which holds that every mother node must have a phonetically non-null constructor.

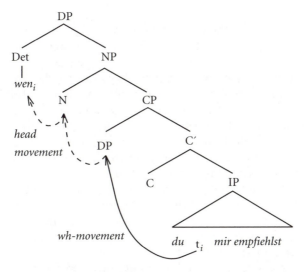

Figure 4.4. The structure of a German free relative. In this tree, the subordinate clause is not adjoined to the maximal DP, but is instead situated within the NP. In this case the wh-phrase moves into the head position.

assigned contradictory feature values, so, given that the two chains formed by the movement transmit the accusative-case feature to the relative pronoun, the entire DP cannot be assigned anything other than accusative case by the matrix verb and yield a grammatical sentence.

For most speakers, the extraposed variants of Example 4.1 are grammatical (Cann and Tait 1990: 25):

(4.9) (a) Ich muss nehmen, wen   du mir   empfiehlst
            I   must take   who(acc) you to me recommend
            'I must take who you recommend to me'

       (b) Ich muss nehmen, wer   einen guten Eindruck   macht
            I   must take   who(nom) a   good impression makes
            'I must take whoever makes a good impression'

       (c) Ich muss nehmen, wem   du vertraust
            I   must take   who(dat) you trust
            'I must take whoever you trust'

Cann and Tait (1990) suggest that the structure of the relatives must be an adjunction structure $_{DP}[DP\ CP]$ (in other words, like the structure in Figure 4.2). It cannot be the same structure as given for the free relatives *in situ,* because moving the CP to the post-verbal position would leave the relative pronoun behind in the clause. Given the same structure as was put forward for non-free relatives, we expect the matching constraint to be impossible and hence the grammaticality of Examples 4.9*a–c.*

The only question remaining is why Cann and Tait (1990) do not propose the adjunction structure for the non-extraposed free relatives (Example 4.7) and instead opt for CP being generated internal to the noun phrase. The answer is rather technical, and only a flavour of it will be given here. Essentially, the phonetic form licensing principle requires that the empty DP_2 in the free relative construction $_{DP_1}[DP_2\ CP]$ be *governed* by the relative clause, CP. Because DP_2 is part of an adjunction structure, the other segment of this structure DP_1 must also be governed. This is not possible if the CP is dominated by DP_1, as it is here. However, if the CP is extraposed then it is available as a governor of both segments of the DP. This problem of government is, on the other hand, not an issue with the structure given in Figure 4.4 because the DP is not empty, and is therefore already phonetically licensed.

In summary, the German free-relative data appear to contradict the explanation given as to why parallel function does not show up cross-linguistically. A closer examination of the syntactic explanations for these language-specific phenomena reveals that this is not the case. The particular idiosyncrasies of the language and/or structure in question may allow the parsing preference to be realized grammatically after all—the status of these findings within the selection model will be considered later in this chapter. For the moment, the message should be that the architecture of grammar cannot be ignored in assessing the cross-linguistic effects of functional pressures. The next section further pushes this message home by uncovering a case where a weight distinction in processing crops up in a different form grammatically. In fact this is a case where the architecture of grammar (i.e. UG) means that the effects of selection are *mal*adaptive.

The English genitive

The prepositional noun-modifier hierarchy of Hawkins (1983) was discussed in Chapter 2. One of the predictions made was that, if a language has variable order at one position of the hierarchy, then it is likely that all modifiers higher on the hierarchy will order one way and the modifiers lower on the hierarchy will order the other way. Modern English exemplifies this nicely, with AdjN and NRel orders and variable order for genitives. The GenN genitive is the so-called Saxon genitive that has survived from Old English, formed by an inflectional suffix on the head noun.

The 'Norman genitive', on the other hand, is formed with a preposition *of* and appears only very rarely in Late Old English (Fischer 1992). The Modern language thus seems to be halfway down the hierarchy:

$$Prep \rightarrow (AdjN > GenN > RelN)$$

The explanation put forward for this effect in Chapter 2 relied on the idea that changes in the orders up the hierarchy happen in sequence and that as a change occurs variant orders may co-occur. In other words, we should expect the prenominal genitive in English to be on the way out, and the postnominal genitive to be on the increase as the language changes its modifier + noun orders in line with its adposition order. If we examine the order of genitives in Middle English, this prediction seems to be cast in doubt. In Middle English, by far the most common genitive construction was NGen, appearing about 85 per cent of the time (Fischer 1992), with the prenominal genitive inherited from Old English as a minor variant. In Modern English, the prenominal genitive is clearly more than a minor variant. The situation is something like:

$$(\text{Middle English})_{\text{GenN}}/\text{NGen} \Rightarrow \text{GenN}/\text{NGen (Modern English)}$$

The order that is dispreferred by EIC—the prenominal genitive—becomes *more* common in Modern English, so it looks less as though the language is simply in transition between two points on the hierarchy. This is especially mystifying when Old English is considered, since GenN was then the predominant order. The order of changes involves an introduction of preferred (from the parsing point of view) order in Modern English and the reduction in frequency of the dispreferred Old English order as expected. In Modern English, however, this trend is reversed with an increase in frequency of GenN. We are left with the question: why has the change turned around?

In order for the selection model to work, it was pointed out in Chapter 2, the variants on which there is a processing pressure must be in competition. Kroch (1994) claims that the situation where grammatical variants are in competition is analogous to the situation where morphological doublets are competing for a paradigm slot. Where the two variants are functionally undifferentiated, then we expect language users to acquire one or other of the two variants at the expense of the other (although the other may exist as a form that is marked in some way). Notice, however, that the condition on competitive replacement by linguistic selection is that the variants are 'functionally undifferentiated'. Kroch (1994: 15–16) gives Dutch adpositions as an example of a case where this condition is not met (examples due to Laura Joosten):

Dutch ... has both prepositions and postpositions. In addition, a number of Dutch adpositions may be either prepositional or postpositional, with, however, a consistent difference in meaning. The prepositions are generally locative, while the postpositions are always directional. The examples below illustrate this behaviour [Kroch's (29)]:

(4.10)   (*a*) Ik fiets in de straat
              I   bike in the street
              (locative only) 'My bike riding takes place in the street'

          (*b*) Ik fiets de straat in
              I   bike the street into
              (directional only) 'My bike riding takes me into the street'

Is it possible that the pre- and post-nominal genitives in Modern English have become functionally differentiated? This would explain why neither form is clearly a 'marked variant' having a kind of 'foreign' status for native speakers as Kroch puts it, and it would also explain why the prenominal form has not continued its expected decline. Wedgwood (1995), discussing this issue, concludes that the two genitive orders are differentiated in Modern English on the basis of the animacy of the modifier. The distribution of the prenominal variant strongly favours animate modifiers, whereas the Saxon genitive appears predominantly with inanimate modifiers:

(4.11)   (*a*) the man's face

          (*b*) ??the clock's face

(4.12)   (*a*) ?the face of the man

          (*b*) the face of the clock

As Wedgwood (1995) points out, linguists vary in the marking of grammaticality of these sorts of examples (e.g. R. Hawkins (1981) and Huddleston (1984) use '?' to suggest gradient acceptability, whereas Giorgi and Longobardi (1991) also use '*' for some sentences). The important point to make about examples such as these is that native speakers have an intuition about this acceptability, and the main determinant of their judgements seems to be the animacy of the modifier. This is not what we might expect given EIC. Instead, we should expect the prenominal genitive to be less acceptable as the *length* of the modifier increases. This is because, in a construction such as $_{PP}[P \; _{NP}[NP \; N]]$, the length of the CRD of PP increases with the length of the genitive noun phrase. Although this is clearly a factor in determining the acceptability of genitive constructions (witness the ready acceptability of *the face of the friendly man next door*), it cannot predict the judgements given above and is incompatible with borderline cases such as:

(4.13)   (a) the friendly man's face

        (b) ?the face of the friendly man

So, animate modifiers are possible prenominally regardless of length, whereas postnominal modifiers will tend to be either inanimate or animate and long. This could mean that there is some processing pressure acting to counter the EIC that prefers animates to be early in the utterance for some reason. We have no reason for believing this at the moment, however, and it is sensible to look for a simpler explanation that does not require us to posit any extra unmotivated psycholinguistic machinery.

Instead, we will simply say that the two types of genitive are functionally differentiated, with the prenominal type 'attracting' animate modifiers. The acceptability judgements given on the basis of animacy are thus not the result of some unknown functional pressure applied on the fly, but instead are coded for as part of native-speaker competence. The form of this coding is debatable, since it does not result in reliable grammaticality judgements—it may be that prenominal genitives with inanimate modifiers are produced as marked variants by analogy with a 'basic' animate variant. This functional differentiation (however it is coded for) stops the process of adaptation, since it does not allow selection to operate on the two genitive orders. The remaining question is whether this differentiation is itself unpredictable or if it too can be related to the adaptive process operating with constraints set by the architecture of grammar.

Limits on grammatical primitives

The parsing theory discussed in Chapter 2 relies on the size in numbers of words of CRDs. This makes sense in terms of parsing and may eventually be reducible to a theory of working memory, the idea being that the amount of information that has to be held in working memory and/or the time for which it has to be held there are directly related to the difficulty in accurately processing that information. This means that processing complexity is a gradient phenomenon which 'counts' numbers of words (cf. Frazier (1985), who puts a discrete limit on the size of 'viewing window' in her parser, and Berwick and Weinberg (1984), whose parser also has an upper bound). This is markedly different from what we see in grammars, which seem unable to count words in this way. In other words the grammar is unable *directly* to reflect processing preferences.

As has been shown, however, there is overwhelming evidence that the grammars of the world's languages *have* responded to parsing. Instead of putting constraints on numbers of words, constraints are placed on positions of syntactic categories, each of which has a different average number of words in texts. In this way, the architecture of grammar forces the acquirer to *reanalyse* patterns in the trigger in terms of category rather than length. So, if a prepositional language has prenominal modifiers, then the parser will filter many of the ModN constructions from the trigger. The likelihood of a construction being well represented in the trigger depends on the number of words in the modifier. The acquisition process cannot capture this generalization, however; instead, the distribution of ModN constructions in the trigger is misanalysed as being dependent on the syntactic category of the modifier. Since relative clauses are likely to be longer than other modifiers, these are most likely to be barred from prenominal position (and so on down the hierarchy). So, all the examples given in this book so far have implicitly assumed some role for constraints on grammatical primitives, otherwise we would expect to find prepositional languages that preposed modifiers less than three words long and postposed others, for example.

Heavy NP shift

Example 4.8 demonstrates a weight-based 'rule' that exemplifies the limits of grammaticalization[6] (from Rickford *et al.* 1995):

(4.14)   (*a*) *bring up it
         (*b*) bring it up
         (*c*) ??bring the subject we were talking about last night up
         (*d*) bring up the subject we were talking about last night

Example 4.14*c* has a long NP interrupting the early processing of the MNCCs of the VP and is hence difficult to process, although we would hesitate to call it ungrammatical. The shifted Example 4.14*d* is much better in comparison. Notice that the shifted Example 4.14*a* is actually ungrammatical. The shift in this case from Example 4.14*b* involves only one word, the pronoun *it*, and therefore brings no advantage in terms of parsing.

---

[6] These are traditionally particle shift examples. The terminology is unimportant, but I will subsume these under the term 'heavy NP shift' because it makes the proposed motivation for the rearrangement clear.

The grammatical situation suggested by these examples is quite complex. In response to pressure from parsing, there seems to be a grammatical variant ordering with the NP shifted rightwards in the VP (the actual syntactic structure of the construction need not concern us here). The non-shifted variant is not ungrammatical, since for many NPs it does not cause a serious problem for parsing. Therefore, both orders must be grammatical because the grammar cannot stipulate a certain number of words above which the NP is too long to stay before the particle. The grammar has responded to the case where the nominal is only a single word by making the postposing of *pronouns* ungrammatical. This is possible since the grammar can make a distinction between pronouns and full NPs. This is a case where a length-based distribution is reanalysed as a category difference, hence the grammaticality of Example 4.15*a–b*, even though the NP is also only a single word:

(4.15)   (*a*) bring up Fred

         (*b*) bring Fred up

All the above is received orthodoxy in linguistics and seems to fit well into the theory of selection constrained by the architecture of grammar. The idea that the occurrence of heavy NP shift in texts is determined by numbers of words in the NP has been challenged, however (see Rickford *et al.* 1995: 117 for a review). Notice, that if we adopt the position of not assuming speaker altruism then we are able to make predictions only about the *acceptability* of the NP-shift sentences, not their distribution in texts. If the latter were determined by weight, then it would mean that speakers were responding to the needs of hearers in shifting NPs.[7]

Rickford *et al.* (1995) present a preliminary statistical study of heavy NP shift in texts and conclude that number of words is not the most significant determinant. Instead they point to a determinant based on the syntactic structure of the NP. According to their results, NPs with embedded sentences are more likely to be shifted, followed by conjoined NPs or NPs containing PPs. Simple NPs with or without modifiers are the least likely to be shifted. From our point of view, there are some problems with this analysis. In order to test the impact of EIC on production of NP shifted sentences we would need to know not only the number of words in the NP, but the number of words in the constituent shifted over. However, that aside, if the syntactic structure of the NP is important, it is interesting to speculate on whether there is a grammatical constraint on

---

[7] It has already been pointed out that the assumption of speaker altruism is not incompatible with the account put forward in this book, but it should not be taken as the null hypothesis.

heavy NP shift after all. Again, it is not clear what form this constraint would take (especially considering it cannot be an exceptionless one), but if this is the case then it demonstrates another way for a grammatical rule to *approximate* to a length-based rule without actually referring to numbers of words.

Animacy and length

Returning to the problem posed by the English genitive construction, it is tempting to consider whether the fixing of the order of animate genitive modifiers prenominally is not also driven by processing. In a prepositional language, the parser prefers genitives to be postnominal, but, if they do appear prenominally, then short genitive modifiers are preferred. The history of the English genitive for a certain period suggests that the pressure from the parser was resulting in the grammaticalization of a postnominal order and the removal of the prenominal genitive. Given the distribution of orders in the trigger (with heavy prenominal genitives tending to be filtered out by the parser), this is the expected response of an acquisition device that is unable to express regularities in the input in terms of numbers of words. Modern English has not continued this trend. Is it possible that the modern language has 'discovered' another way of expressing the processing preference apparent in the trigger experience—one that differentiates between GenN and NGen in a way that reflects the relative lengths of the two types of modifier? This boils down to whether animates tend to be shorter than inanimates.

In order to answer this question Wedgwood (1995) looks at the lengths of relevant animate and inanimate genitive modifiers in a random sample from the LOB corpus of present-day English.

A 'relevant genitive' is here taken to be some attributive relation between two nouns using (in one sample) the *of-* and (in the other) the *-'s* constructions, which, except for the differentiation by animacy, is potentially expressible using either construction.   (Wedgwood 1995: 23)

The genitives are then split into two categories on the basis of the animacy of the modifier and their length distribution recorded. The results are reproduced in Table 4.1 (Wedgwood 1995: 24). This distribution shows that, statistically, animates are significantly shorter than inanimates.

The picture that results from this is that, at some point in the history of English, the parser-imposed distribution of genitive modifiers (short genitives prenominally) was reanalysed by language acquirers as reflecting a preference for animates prenominally. This is understandable, since the longer modifiers that would be filtered out in prenominal position were more likely to be inanimate. This animacy distinction can be expressed by the grammar, whereas length cannot, so the two types of genitive became

Table 4.1. *Length distribution by animacy*

Type of genitive	Length										
	1	2	3	4	5	6	7	8	9	10	>10
Animate	103	98	12	4	2	1	0	2	0	1	1
Inanimate	15	72	40	11	12	5	1	2	2	0	3

functionally differentiated on the basis of animacy. Now it is impossible for selection to continue to work, since the two genitives are no longer in competition in Kroch's (1994) terms. Interestingly enough, the selective process, constrained as it was by possible grammatical primitives, fails to result in the 'perfect' adaptation (only allowing NGen), and the possibility of long prenominal animate genitives is retained.

If the length difference between animates and inanimates could be shown to be universal, then we can make an interesting prediction about precedence rules in languages that make a grammatical distinction based on animacy. We should find at least in a significant number of cases that the order of animates versus inanimates follows the order of heads and modifiers in the language. Although such a study is beyond the scope of this work, it is interesting to note that Morolong and Hyman (1977, cited in Hawkins 1994a: 424) describe a rule in Sesotho grammar which mirrors the English genitive case. If dative and patient noun phrases are both animate or both inanimate they may appear in either order in the Sesotho clause. Where they differ in animacy, the animate comes first. Given that Sesotho constituents are recognized on their left boundary, it is more efficient for long noun phrases to appear late to minimize recognition domains. This appears to be grammaticalized in terms of animacy. Further work needs to be done in this interesting area, particularly to check if head final languages with animacy-based rules tend to order animates late.

A final example involves German datives and accusatives. Consider the following sentences:

(4.16) (*a*) Ich gab es   ihm
            I   gave it(acc) him(dat)
            'I gave it to him'

        (*b*) ?Ich gab ihm   es
            I   gave him(dat) it(acc)

(4.17) (*a*) ?Ich gab das Buch   ihm
            I   gave the book(acc) him(dat)

(b) Ich gab ihm   das Buch
      I   gave him(dat) the book(acc)

(c) ?Ich gab dem Mann   es
      I   gave the man(dat) it(acc)

(d) Ich gab es   dem Mann
      I   gave it(acc) the man(dat)

(4.18) (a) ?Ich gab das Buch   dem Mann
             I   gave the book(acc) the man(dat)

         (b) Ich gab dem Mann   das Buch
             I   gave the man(dat) the book(acc)

Example 4.16a–b shows that, where both dative and accusative are of minimal length (i.e. pronouns), there is an arbitrary grammaticalized ordering principle for accusative first.[8] However, when one of the nominals is a full noun phrase and the other is a pronoun, parsing considerations have been grammaticalized so that the pronoun is strongly preferred before the noun phrase (Example 4.17a–d). Finally, where both nominals are full noun phrases, and hence could potentially vary in length considerably, the preferred order is dative before accusative. James Hurford (personal communication) has suggested that this may be because datives are typically more animate than accusatives and, as we have already shown, animates are on average shorter than inanimates. Hence, these examples show two ways in which a short-before-long parsing preference has been grammaticalized in German: first, based on the difference in prototypical lengths of pronouns versus full noun phrases, and secondly based on the difference in prototypical animacy of dative and accusative, and, derivatively, their lengths.

Implications of constraints on adaptation for linguistic theory

The discussion in this chapter has highlighted the importance of examining both processing considerations and formal models of syntax in explaining the origin of language universals. Both the parser and the innate LAD leave their mark on language, but it is only by taking into consideration both mechanisms that the role of each can be uncovered. The diagram in Figure 4.5 shows the different possible classes of language. *E* is the set of logically possible languages; *L* is the class of learnable languages, its

---

[8] Although notice that there is the same problem here as with the English genitive examples regarding the judgement of ungrammaticality.

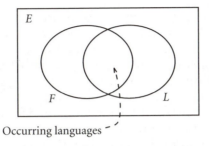

Figure 4.5. Interacting constraints on possible languages.

boundary set by the innate LAD; and *F* is the class of languages predicted to occur given the selection theory of Chapters 2 and 3. Obviously, the languages we should expect to occur are those in $F \cap L$. Some of the languages predicted by the application of parallel function to the selection model do not occur because they are in the set $F \cap \overline{L}$. Similarly there may be languages that do not occur but are perfectly learnable in the set $\overline{F} \cap L$. These are ruled out by considerations of processing. I would argue that many of the language types that are barred by the universals considered in this book are in this set. So, for example, a language with oblique relatives but no direct object relatives is ruled out because of the interaction of p- and m-complexity in the arena of use. There is nothing that should lead us to believe that such a language is actually unlearnable.

This diagram fails to capture some of the more subtle interactions discussed here, however. We have seen that (*a*) languages *can* arise that respond to parallel function, albeit in unexpected ways, and (*b*) the animacy distinction in the English genitive is explicable in terms of processing, although the outcome does not fit into the general pattern of adaptation. The acquisition device in a sense provides *ad hoc* solutions to the problem of representing in I-language the pressure exerted by processing on E-language. What these 'solutions' will be is fairly predictable, although sometimes the outcome is unexpected. In the English case there was a reanalysis of the underlying regularities in the input data—a length difference was reinterpreted using the grammatical primitive, animacy.

The processing mechanisms make selections among utterances, and those selections cannot inform the acquisition device except by filtering input from the trigger. The resulting changes in the grammar of the language may lead to the removal of the particular structures that cause problems for processing, but they may not. If we are to gain a deeper understanding of the origins of universals we need to look for all the processing pressures that might be involved *and* what role the effect of those pressures on the trigger might play in the process of acquisition. The advantage of this approach is that troublesome counter-examples from the functional perspective may be mitigated by looking into constraints imposed by the architecture of grammar; from another perspective the burden of explaining all constraints on distribution uncovered by typology can be lifted from a theory of the structure of an innate UG.

We are now at a point where the functional and formal (or innatist) perspectives are mutually reinforcing, rather than competing, as they appear to be from so much of the literature (see Hurford 1990 for review). The recourse to innate/formal constraints might seem to raise more questions than it answers. For example, can the particulars of a formal theory of UG themselves be derived from other factors, or are they mere stipulations set up to account for the data? The emerging field of evolutionary linguistics suggests that functional considerations may directly influence the structure of the innate language faculty. The next chapter considers this final thread in the web of function, selection, and innateness.

5   Innateness and Function in Linguistics

It is widely believed by linguists that the human ability to acquire language is at least in some part innately given, and that UG in the Chomskyan sense is embodied in this ability. Indeed, this assumption has been implicit in much of the discussion in this book so far. The previous chapter showed that such an innate LAD is required in combination with a theory of linguistic selection in order fully to understand the fit of universals to processing pressures. Recent research has begun to look at the possibility of examining the origins of the features of this innate faculty themselves, arguing that these too may have their roots in essentially functional pressures. This final chapter reviews some of this recent literature and examines whether it poses a competing theory of the origin of universals.

Natural selection and the LAD

Christiansen (1994) characterizes explanations of the origin of an innate LAD into two types: *exaptationist* and *adaptationist*. Proponents of the first type of explanation—among whom Christiansen cites Chomsky (1988)[1] and Piattelli-Palmerini (1989)—argue that natural selection plays only a minor role in the evolution of the complex domain-specific LAD. Instead, the term *exaptation* (Gould and Vrba 1982) is used to describe the mechanism whereby the neural structures supporting language acquisition evolve. Exaptation refers to the reappropriation of form for some purpose other than the one that drove its evolution. Indeed Gould and Lewontin (1979) admit the possibility that the structure that is exapted may have no prior function at all, but simply be a 'spandrel'.[2] In this view, then, the LAD might simply be a by-product of increased brain size, for example.

---

[1] The views of Chomsky on the evolution of language are notoriously difficult to unravel. In some papers he seems to suggest that the LAD can be viewed from an adaptationist perspective (e.g. Chomsky and Lasnik 1977; Chomsky 1980). A complete review of his views on this point would be a major undertaking, however see Newmeyer's (1994*b*) for an interesting perspective.

[2] The term 'spandrel' is an architectural one, referring to a space formed at the meeting of two arches. At the San Marco basilica in Venice these spandrels are filled with a mosaic design which perfectly fits the triangular space provided. Gould and Lewontin point out that this apparent design should not lead us to believe that the function of the arch is to provide the artist with a space for a mosaic. Instead the spandrel is a by-product of the arch which has been adapted, or *exapted*, for an artistic function.

The adaptationist perspective (e.g. Hurford 1989, 1991; Pinker and Bloom 1990) places the burden of explaining the origin of the LAD on natural selection. In particular the LAD is claimed to have evolved through selection *for the function it now fulfils*. This relies on the assumption that human language confers a survival or reproductive advantage on the organisms that have it. This assumption seems to be fairly well accepted, although when we get to specific features of UG (see below) there seems to be greater unease. Lightfoot (1991: 69), for example, pours scorn on the adaptationist argument, suggesting 'the Subjacency Condition has many virtues, but I am not sure that it could have increased the chances of having fruitful sex'. We should reject Lightfoot's complaint because it relies on the 'argument from personal incredulity', in Richard Dawkin's words. It rejects the adaptationist position simply because it is hard to believe, but where is the alternative? That the LAD evolved as an adaptation to acquisition should be our null-hypothesis—after all, natural selection is the most successful explanation of adapted complexity in nature that we have—so the burden is on the exaptationists to come up with an alternative explanation. (We will return to the specific problem of subjacency later.)

Of course, before we appeal to the adaptationist approach, we need to know in what way the LAD is *adaptive*.

Do the cognitive mechanisms underlying language show signs of design for some function in the same way the anatomical structures of the eye show signs of design for the purpose of vision? What are the engineering demands on a system that must carry out such a function? And are the mechanisms of language tailored to meet those demands?   (Pinker and Bloom 1990: 712)

To begin to answer these questions, and bolster support for the idea that the LAD is an adaptation, Pinker and Bloom (1990: 713–14) list some design features of grammars such as: major and minor lexical categories, major phrasal categories, phrase structure rules, linear order rules, case affixes, verb affixes, auxiliaries, anaphoric elements, complementation, control, and wh-movement. They claim that these features of grammars—which from our innatist perspective are properties of the LAD—work together to make 'communication of propositional structures' possible. Notice that Pinker and Bloom are not talking about the particular instantiations of these features in languages, but their existence as features of language as a whole. So, for example, linear order and case affixes 'distinguish among the argument positions that an entity assumes with respect to a predicate' (p. 713), suggesting that their presence in UG requires an adaptationist explanation. However, notice that the *particular* word orders or case affixes found in languages are not an issue for Pinker and Bloom.

The general features of UG appear to be one possible evolutionary solution to the problem of acquiring and representing a communicative system that allows the transmission of propositional structures. This adaptationist argument does not exclude a role for exaptation. Hurford and Kirby (1995) commenting on Wilkins and Wakefield (1995) suggest that a faculty for some form of *proto-language* (Bickerton 1990) was a primate exaptation from neural structures serving mental representation, but the human LAD has adapted from this precursor. In a sense, any exaptationist argument must include some degree of adaptation, since it is highly improbable that a complex structure evolved to fulfil some function can, by coincidence, also be used for some other purpose. The real issue is at what point in evolutionary history the LAD began to evolve in response to pressures imposed by the function it now fulfils. To put it another way, how much of the current LAD can we ascribe to natural selection for linguistic communication? Pinker and Bloom's argument suggests that at least some of the most basic features of UG are adaptations for communicative purposes.

Newmeyer on function

If we accept the idea that the origin of the LAD necessarily involves some degree of adaptation to the function it currently fulfils, and furthermore that the 'basic design features' of Pinker and Bloom (1990) are the result of this adaptation, we are led to an interesting conclusion about more specific features of UG. Since the adaptation of the LAD to communicative ends must occur after any exaptation of neural structures, the more specific to language a mental feature is the more likely it is to be the result of an adaptation. The fact that, say, the presence of linear order rules are an adaptation to communicative ends suggests that the subjacency principle, for example, must also be viewed as an adaptation. To say otherwise would be to suggest that the subjacency principle is a leftover from some other neural function whereas the presence of linear ordering in language is not, yet no non-linguistic parallel of subjacency has been proposed but it is easy to think of non-linguistic domains in which linear ordering is important (in the formulation of plans, for example).

Autonomy

This common-sense argument raises the obvious challenge of explaining the specific architecture of a Chomskyan UG in terms of adaptation to the function of communication. Rather surprisingly, given the repeated claims of Chomsky that UG is innate and the demonstrated success of neo-Darwinian explanations of biological complexity, this challenge has until recently been ignored. Part of the reason may be that adaptationist explanations appear to be at odds with the *assumption of the autonomy of syntax*, which states that 'there exists a set of nonsemantic and nondiscourse-derived grammatical primitives whose principles of combination make no reference to system-external factors' (Newmeyer 1992: 783; see also Chomsky 1975). In other words, an autonomous syntactic component will make no use of information about external functional pressures nor will it include representations of those pressures.

This assumption, although allowing generative syntactic theory to progress rapidly, has unfortunately caused linguists interested in functional explanation generally to reject generative syntax and some of those who accept the autonomy thesis to deny the possibility of functional explanation. This rejection of the link between function and autonomy is misguided in two ways.

First, the simulations presented in this book explicitly take on board the assumption of autonomy in the design of the data structures that encode grammars. As discussed in Chapter 2, they have purposefully been made as simple as possible: mere lists of possible utterance types. In no sense does the I-domain have any access to information about the processing complexity of the utterances they indirectly encode. Nevertheless, the universals that emerge from the simulations clearly have a functional explanation. The end state of the simulation is that the particular distribution of grammars of the speech community collectively encode the processing pressures in the arena of use, without ever violating the autonomy of the individual grammatical knowledge of the language users. Furthermore, the evidence presented in Chapter 4 *requires* the autonomy assumption for the functional explanation to work.

Secondly, as Newmeyer (1991) argues, functional considerations may directly shape the form of the syntactic component without violating its autonomy from function:

Despite the frequently voiced functionalist opinion that to identify a principle as innate is to abandon any attempt to explain it, there exists a well-accepted (functional) mechanism for explaining the provenance of innate traits: natural selection. It is quite plausible that the design of the grammatical model as a whole or *some particular grammatical principle* might have become encoded in our genes by virtue of its being successful in facilitating communication that the survival and reproductive possibilities of those possessing it were enhanced. In a sense, a functional explanation would hold at the evolutionary level.

Thus autonomy is also compatible with a functional explanation for those aspects of language that form part of our biological endowment.   (Newmeyer 1991: 7, emphasis added)

Thus Newmeyer is going further than Pinker and Bloom in espousing a functional explanation for particular features of UG, rather than the

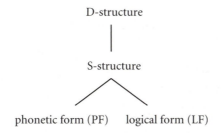

Figure 5.1. The polystratal architecture of the GB theory of syntax.

broader design features of language. He also appears to admit the possibility that the same pressures that are appealed to by functional linguists can be applied to phylogenetic explanation.

Polystratal models of syntax and iconicity

The standard structure of the government-binding theory of syntax is shown in Figure 5.1. The syntactic structure of a sentence is simultaneously represented at the various levels in the diagram which are related by a declarative transformational rule, move-α, whose role is to relate elements in particular positions at one level with the 'same' elements in different positions at neighbouring levels.[3]

This polystratal representation schema is part of the autonomous, innately given, architecture of grammar, but Newmeyer (1992) argues that it can be given a functional explanation in terms of *iconicity* (e.g. Haiman 1985). Givón (1985) suggests that a syntactic *form* is easier to process if it is in an iconic relation with its *content*, if 'the code is maximally isomorphic to the experience' (p. 189). If this is true, then we can expect that grammatical representations will be arranged in such a way as to favour iconicity. There are, however, many ways in which a form can be iconic, reflecting the several dimensions of 'content'.

Maximal isomorphism for one property may not be maximal isomorphism for another. Consider, for example [Newmeyer's (32)]:

(5.1) (*a*) Who did Mary love?

  (*b*) Mary loved everyone.

  (*c*) Mary loved John.

---

[3] Recent developments in generative syntax (e.g. Chomsky 1993; Marantz 1995) have suggested a revision to this model involving a more derivational approach to move-α, and only two levels, although it is possible that this could be given a declarative interpretation with multiple levels. We will not discuss this here, but Newmeyer's discussion is probably consistent with this variant of the model.

These three sentences have identical predicate-argument relations; their D-structure representations are thus identical, roughly as in [Newmeyer's (33)]:

(5.2)   (*a*) Mary loved who.

(*b*) Mary loved everyone.

(*c*) Mary loved John.

But at the level at which [Examples 5.1*a–c*] are represented identically, it is not easy to capture in any elegant way the fact that the quantification relations in [Examples 5.1*a–b*] differ profoundly from those in [Example 5.1*c*], which is not an operator-bound variable construction semantically.   (Newmeyer 1992: 788–9)

So, we have a conflict here between an iconic representation of predicate-argument relations and quantifier-variable relations. Both cannot be represented in an iconic fashion at the same level. Instead, the former is represented at D-structure as above, and the later at LF as (Newmeyer 1992: 788):

(5.3)   (*a*) Who$_i$ [Mary love e$_i$]

(*b*) Everyone$_i$ [Mary love e$_i$]

(*c*) Mary love John

The word order of utterances may not always reflect one or other of these levels partly because of considerations of processing such as heavy constituent shift. This motivates the presence of a the third level, S-structure (Newmeyer does not discuss PF).

Polystratal representations of syntactic structure as part of our biologically given faculty for language have arisen for functional reasons during the evolution of our species. The pressure for iconic representations—ultimately in response to processing needs—has favoured syntactic structures in which the 'same' elements (i.e. elements that are related by move-α) can enter into different iconic relations at different levels. In this way, Newmeyer approaches a basic assumption of autonomous syntax from a functional perspective.

Principles and processing

In another important paper Newmeyer (1991) goes further with the idea that processing can ultimately explain the nature of many of the specific principles of UG, also without compromising the autonomy thesis.

We have already seen that the model of autonomous grammar . . . has features that suggest it was shaped by natural selection, that is, that it evolved to its present state in effect *because* it was functionally so advantageous. It will be argued . . . that the same is true of the central principles of autonomous syntax. These principles were encoded in our genes by virtue of their playing such a central role in communication that the survival and reproductive possibilities of the species were advanced as a result of them.   (Newmeyer 1991: 12)

One of the examples that Newmeyer gives is Subjacency (Riemsdijk and Williams 1986: 62, cited in Newmeyer 1991: 12):

Subjacency condition.   No rule can relate X, Y in the structure

$$\ldots X \ldots [\alpha \ldots [\beta \ldots Y \ldots$$

or

$$\ldots Y \ldots]\beta \ldots]\alpha \ldots X \ldots$$

where α, β are bounding nodes.

In English, the bounding nodes are IP and NP, hence the ungrammaticality of the sentences in Example 5.4, where *who* has moved over two bounding nodes (with no intermediate 'landing site'[4]):

(5.4)   (*a*)   *I met the fan who$_i$ we played $_{NP}$[the song which$_j$ $_{IP}$[t_i liked t_j]]

(*b*)   *Who$_i$ did $_{IP}$[Matt tell you when$_j$ $_{IP}$[he had met $t_i t_j$]]

The standard assumption is that the subjacency condition is one of a set of constraints on the application of move-α that form part of our innate knowledge of language. Although there is some cross-linguistic variability in the inventory of bounding nodes, the constraint can, in principle, be applied to any language. How can the existence of this constraint be explained? Berwick and Weinberg (1984) point out that the subjacency condition tends to rule out sentences in which the distance between the wh-element and its co-indexed gap is long. As already discussed in Chapter 4, there is a pressure from the parser to keep this distance to a minimum. Newmeyer's argument is that this parsing pressure led to the biological selection of an LAD that had some way of eliminating the worst wh-extractions from the language. Crucially, the resultant constraint does not make any reference to parsability, or even distance, but is an autonomous principle which tends to rule out particularly long-distance movement.[5]

Newmeyer (1991: 13) goes on to suggest that Principle A of the binding theory and the empty category principle have similar functional motivations. They both constrain the syntactic positions of anaphoric elements

---

[4]   See e.g. Haegeman (1991: §6.2) for further details of the applicability of the subjacency condition.

[5]   We will review other perspectives on the subjacency condition later in this chapter.

and their antecedents, which suggests that they may also aid the parsing of co-indexed elements. Newmeyer, however, does not go into this parsing motivation in any detail, so these principles will not be discussed here. Suffice to say that both principles also do not make reference to 'system-external factors', even though an explanation of their origin can be conceived in terms of parsing pressures.

The LAD and universals

The previous section sketched a view of functional explanation that is rather different from the one put forward in this book. Various design features of the LAD and innate principles appear to show the kind of evidence of fit that was introduced in Chapter 1. But, this 'appearance of design' is precisely what we observed in the universals of previous chapters. Is it possible, then, that the phylogenetic approach to explanation proposed by Newmeyer can be extended to cover the same universals that have been the focus of this book—for example, the word-order universals of Chapter 2? This type of explanation would be available to us only if we assumed that the word-order universals we have looked at resulted from some innate constraint. This is in contradiction to what has been assumed so far, amounting to changing Figure 4.5 so that the area $\overline{F} \cap L$ (non-functional, learnable languages) is reduced to $\emptyset$ (see Figure 5.2).

As discussed in Chapter 2, one of the universals that Hawkins's (1994a) theory attempts to explain is the tendency for languages to have a consistent positioning of head relative to non-heads across phrasal categories. How might this be accounted for in terms of innate UG? As Giorgi and Longobardi (1991) point out, the development of X-bar theory (e.g. Jackendoff 1977) allowed for this regularity to be expressed as

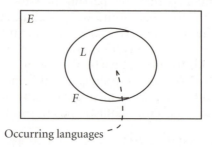

Occurring languages

Figure 5.2. Possible languages where universals are explained exclusively by a functionally motivated LAD.

a generalization over phrase structure rules, so that the rules specifying the order of head and complement can be expressed as $X' \rightarrow X\ XP$ or $X' \rightarrow XP\ X$, with X ranging over the set of lexical categories. Later, after Stowell's (1981) rejection of phrase-structure rules, Chomsky (1986: 88) simply refers to a 'head-complement parameter' which can be either *head final* or *head initial* for a particular language.

Obviously, the problem with this approach to the universal is that there are exceptions to the generalization—not all languages are consistently head initial or head final, although they *tend* to pattern that way. Travis (1984) looks at the word order of Modern Mandarin with respect to the head-complement parameter. She points out that NPs are head final, and certain PPs appear preverbally, also suggesting that the parameter is set to head final. However, some PPs and direct object NPs can appear to the right of the verb. Furthermore, Modern Mandarin has prepositions rather than postpositions. For example (Travis 1984: 46, from Li and Thompson 1975: 180):

(5.5)   (*a*) ta gei wo mai le   chezi le
             he for me sell ASP car   ASP
             'He sold a car for me'

      (*b*) ta mai gei wo chezi le
             he sell to me car   ASP
             'He sold a car to me'

Example 5.5*a* contains a pre-verbal benefactive PP, whereas Example 5.5*b* contains a post-verbal dative PP. Travis (1984: 48–53) argues at length that the difference between these types of PP can best be characterized as a difference in the assignment of the θ-role to *wo*. In the post-verbal case, she argues that the θ-role is assigned by the verb, whereas in the pre-verbal case the θ-role is assigned by the preposition. She then goes on to propose another parameter governing word order:

the direction of θ-role assignment is another parameter which determines word order in languages. We can claim that while [Modern Mandarin] is head final, it assigns θ-roles to the right. If we look at the two categories that assign θ-roles, prepositions and verbs, we see that both of them appear to the left of the NPs to which they assign θ-roles. We will assume that within NPs, θ-roles are assigned by the preposition and not by the head N.   (Travis 1984: 53–4)

Only a flavour of Travis's account can be provided here, but she goes on to include another directional parameter: that of case assignment. In this way different settings of the parameters can account for all possible orders of the two types of PP, and direct objects relative to the verb. This is because neither type of PP is case marked by the verb, but the direct object is. So the case-assignment parameter may control the position of the direct object in relation to the verb independently of that of the PPs.

Where does that leave the observation that languages *tend* to pattern as head initial or head final? First, notice that the head-ordering parameter can be in conflict with the other parameters. For Modern Mandarin, the head-ordering parameter defines the default ordering of constituents, but the setting of the θ-marking parameter overrides this for the object and θ-marked PP. It could be argued, then, that all we need to account for the distribution of languages is for the contradictory setting of parameters to be marked in some way. Giorgi and Longobardi (1991: 151) also argue that marked settings of parameters can account for cross-linguistic patterns, although they are looking at word order within the NP.

In summary, the innate LAD builds grammars with consistent head ordering as a default, but the setting of other parameters relating to the assignment of θ-roles and case may override these settings in the marked case. Stepping into Newmeyer's shoes, we might now say that the reason that UG is set up this way—that is, with default consistent head ordering—is because of parsing. The EIC preferences for consistent ordering of MNCCs in this view influence the biological evolution of the LAD in order to constrain languages to aid parsing.

Biologization or grammaticalization?

Finally, we have come full circle: the cross-linguistic universals have been explained ultimately with reference to parsing. The problem is that there are now two candidate explanations for the same observed fit between universals and processing—a glossogenetic one in which languages themselves adapt to the pressures of transmission through the arena of use, and a phylogenetic one in which the LAD adapts to the pressures of survival in an environment where successful communication is advantageous. Looking at Figure 5.3, we can see that, if we accept Pinker and Bloom's (1990) approach, the difference between the functionalist and innatist positions is not in what explains language universals, but in the approach to solving the *problem of linkage.*

Subjacency five ways

Further to highlight the lack of clarity in the literature regarding the connection between function, innateness, and universals, we can return once again to the subjacency condition. At least five different positions are discernible on the issue of what this principle tells us about function and UG.

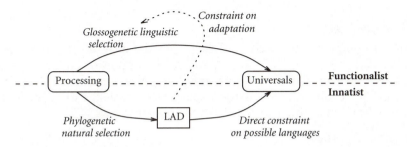

Figure 5.3. The (adaptive) innatist and functionalist approaches as solutions to the problem of linkage.

Piattelli-Palmerini (1989)

As already discussed, this author presents an exaptationist viewpoint on the emergence of the LAD. Part of the basis for his argument is the observation of *arbitrariness* in the formulation of UG principles (such as subjacency). The specific substance of the principle is not predictable as an adaptation to communication, therefore it lacks the appearance of design that is so typical of structures evolving through natural selection.

Pinker and Bloom (1990)

In these authors' view, Piattelli-Palmerini's (1989) argument is flawed, since there is nothing about evolution by natural selection that rules out arbitrariness. This is particularly true if communication is considered. The very nature of communication requires a shared coding protocol which may well be arbitrarily chosen from a set of equally functional options. Just because the specific principles that are innately coded cannot be predicted by looking at function, this does not mean that natural selection has not shaped those principles. Specifically, they argue that subjacency is an *arbitrary* compromise solution to pressures from expressiveness and parsing. 'In the evolution of the language faculty, many "arbitrary" constraints may have been selected simply because they defined parts of a standardized communicative code in the brains of a critical mass of speakers' (Pinker and Bloom 1990: 718).

The subjacency condition could have been nativized in some other form, but to them the crucial point is that it must have been nativized somehow. In support of this, they cite Mayr (1982: 612) on communication elsewhere in biology:

Behaviour that serves communication, for instance courtship behaviour, must be stereotyped in order not to be misunderstood. The genetic program controlling such behaviour must be 'closed', that is, it must be reasonably resistant to any changes during the individual life cycle . . .

Newmeyer (1991)

This viewpoint has been covered earlier in the chapter. It differs from Pinker and Bloom's mainly with regard to the importance placed on the parsability of subjacency-violating structures. Newmeyer also stresses the pressure for evolution to constrain speakers of language in order to aid hearers—an issue which we will return to shortly.

Christiansen (1994)

Whereas Newmeyer, and to a lesser extent Pinker and Bloom, use the heavy parsing complexity of subjacency-violating structures as evidence for the biological evolution of the constraint, Christiansen instead uses the same observation as evidence *against* an innate subjacency condition.

> Since we therefore reasonably can construe subjacency simply as a constraint on processing ... it can no longer be considered to be an arbitrary linguistic phenomenon (as suggested by Pinker and Bloom 1990), but must indeed be conceived as a nonarbitrary byproduct of limited human processing abilities.   (Christiansen 1994: 130)

Notice that Christiansen appears to have missed the fact that Pinker and Bloom themselves appeal to the same evidence he does (i.e. the observations of Berwick and Weinberg 1984) to argue the opposite view.

Hawkins (1994a)

The final viewpoint on subjacency is rather different from the others here, since it rejects the existence of the condition altogether. Instead, Hawkins proposes a wh-extraction hierarchy, where each position on the hierarchy involves a movement spanning a larger structural domain than the positions higher on the hierarchy. Languages select positions on this hierarchy above which wh-extraction is grammatical, and below which it is not, in response to pressure from the parser.

Hawkins's argument against the classical interpretation of subjacency is based on a rejection of the 'comp-to-comp' analysis of apparent violations of the condition. In this view, movements which appear to straddle two or more bounding nodes in fact take place in multiple stages, with the wh-element stopping off in intermediate positions (compare with Example 5.4*b*):

(5.6) Who$_i$ did $_{IP}$[Matt tell you $_{CP}$[t_i that $_{IP}$[he had met t_i]]]

Here, the wh-element has moved from the lower [Spec,CP] to the higher [Spec,CP] and neither move violates the subjacency condition by crossing two IP nodes. Hawkins (1994*a*) rejects this approach because of the lack of any independent psycholinguistic motivation for it. Notice, however, that it is just this kind of (partial) arbitrariness that other authors have used to argue for the innateness of the subjacency condition.

Speaker altruism again

At the moment it is a difficult task to choose between the five points of view summarized above, in the specific case of subjacency and in the general approaches to innateness and function that they suggest. The work presented in this book can shed light on some of the issues raised, however.

The evidence presented in Chapter 4 should lead us to be wary of any approach that rejects an autonomous innate component altogether. In other words, there must be some *biologization* of functional pressures involved, because the linguistic-selection approach simply cannot explain the universals on its own. If this is the case, we might wonder if there has been any glossogenetic adaptation at all.

One of the crucial features of Newmeyer's (1991) approach is his rejection of just this sort of glossogenetic functional explanation for language universals. He relies on an implicit rejection of speaker altruism in order to make his point:

In cases where ease for the speaker and the requirements of the hearer were in direct conflict, an obvious solution presented itself—to bypass directly the push–pull between speakers' demands and hearers' demands by incorporating those constraints necessary to the hearer directly into the innate language faculty itself. Thus the principles of UG were selected for, allowing a stable innate core to language, immune to the functional exigencies of the moment.   (Newmeyer 1991: 15)

In this way, Newmeyer rejects the possibility of particular languages evolving over a historical timescale to pressures from the parser. *If* speakers are not altruistic, he suggests, then there is no way in which hearers' needs could be reflected in grammars. And yet, subjacency (and indeed many of the universals we have discussed) appear to reflect just such one-sided needs. Hence, Newmeyer argues, they must have evolved phylogenetically.

Though there are certainly some innate constraints on acquisition that will ultimately be explained by appealing to functional asymmetries, it is a mistake to suggest that there will be a biological response wherever there is such a speaker/hearer difference. The simulations of Chapters 2 and 3 show that languages may adapt glossogenetically to an asymmetric functional pressure, through a process of linguistic selection by the parser, even where there is not an innate constraint on them to do so. This weakens Newmeyer's argument considerably; linguistic selection and natural selection are both still, in principle, capable of explaining principles such as subjacency.

A more rewarding approach I would argue would be to admit the possibility of both kinds of adaptation and examine the mechanisms involved in more detail. It certainly seems likely given the quite different nature of the processes and objects that play a part in *biologization* and *grammaticalization*[6] that they will have observable differences once they are better understood. This book has gone some way to explore the glossogenetic adaptation and to provide a sufficiently general and explanatory account of the universals examined in terms of linguistic selection. In as much as this has been successful, this should lead us to reject arguments that the universals thus explained, such as the tendency for consistent head-ordering, have an innate basis.

An approach to modelling the evolution of language

On the other hand, a similar investigation into modelling natural selection in language evolution (see Steels 1997 for a review of the general field) might lead to an explanation of those universals that are more difficult for the linguistic-selection approach. In this category we might put subjacency whose partially adaptive, partially arbitrary, characteristics are highlighted by Pinker and Bloom (1990), and also those constraints discussed in the previous chapter whose existence is predicted by 'failures' of glossogenetic adaptation.

What might such a model look like? More specifically, how would it counter Lightfoot's (1991) sceptical conclusion that the subjacency condition could not improve breeding success? A particularly promising line of work resurrects an evolutionary principle of Baldwin (1896), referred to as the Baldwin Effect. This effect predicts that a population of organisms that learn a beneficial behavioural pattern will tend, over time, to nativize that pattern. As French and Messinger (1994) note, the Baldwin Effect is still far from uncontroversial in biology, possibly because of its apparent similarity to Lamarkian evolutionary principles; however, in an important paper, Hinton and Nowlan (1987) show that the effect is completely compatible with neo-Darwinian assumptions.

Hinton and Nowlan examine the evolutionary dynamics of a population of organisms each with a set of twenty 'neurons' which may be in one of two states. Each organism has a genotype that is made up of twenty genes, each of which has three possible alleles: 1, 0, or ?. The first two possibilities directly code for a corresponding neuron's state in that organism. The ? allele, on the other hand leaves the state of the corresponding neuron open to learning. The fitness of each organism (i.e. its chance of procreating) corresponds to the states of its neurons in such a way that for an organism

---

[6] *Grammaticalization* is used in the sense introduced in Chapter 2.

to increase its fitness it must have *exactly the right set of neuronal states*. In other words, having only one neuron set wrong is just as bad as having all twenty wrong. The fitness landscape of this problem can be envisaged as a flat (hyper-)plane with a single spike in it. Natural selection on its own has little chance of finding this spike; indeed it is no better than a random search at finding the 1 in 1,048,576 lucky individual with increased fitness.

The inclusion of the ? alleles, however, makes all the difference. In the Hinton and Nowlan simulation, learning is implemented by an organism being allowed to try 1,000 random settings of its neurons correspond-ing to ? alleles. If one of these attempts results in a correct setting of all twenty neurons (i.e. in combination with the neurons that are genetically specified), then this learning process stops. The chances of each organism being chosen as a parent in the creation of the next generation of organ-isms (which involves a simple recombination of genomes to create new individuals) depends on how quickly it reached the adaptive configura-tion.[7] Importantly, the learned settings of neurons are not passed on to the next generation (which would entail Lamarkian evolution); rather, it is the sequence of 1, 0, and ? that is used to form the offspring.

The original population of organisms each have on average ten learnable neuronal settings, and five each of the pre-set 1s and 0s. During the simu-lation, the alleles specifying incorrect settings quickly disappear from the population, and the number of ? alleles decreases. As Hinton and Nowlan put it, learning has guided evolution. The reason for the relative success of nativizing the correct settings when learning is involved, is due to the change in fitness landscape that the inclusion of ? alleles brings about. In the case where learning is not available, an organism near the correct com-bination is no fitter than one far away, but, with the inclusion of learning, the landscape is *smoothed* so that an organism near the fitness peak is fitter (in the sense of being able to get to the top more quickly) than one that is far away.

This effect has been elaborated in simulations by a number of researchers looking at various behaviours such as food finding (e.g. Nolfi *et al.* 1994), carnivore avoidance (e.g. Ackley and Littman 1991), and even the evo-lution of (non-linguistic) communication (e.g. MacLennan 1991). In all these cases the ability of an organism to learn can guide evolution up to the peak of a fitness landscape. This highlights an attractive feature of

---

[7] The fitness μ of an individual $x_i \in (0\ 1\ ?)^L$ is a function of the number of learning attempts made g:

$$\mu(x_i(g)) = 1 + \frac{(L-1)(G-g)}{G}$$

where G is the maximum number of learning attempts allowed (here 1,000). See Belew (1990) for an accessible analysis of the Hinton and Nowlan (1987) simulation.

the Baldwin Effect from our perspective. A common complaint regarding studies of the evolution of the human-language faculty is that it is difficult to imagine a *gradual* evolution of the complex set of interacting constraints and principles that make up our language faculty. Such a faculty seems to us to be a 'fitness spike', since, without one component, how could the whole function at all? The simulations of the Baldwin Effect show that just such a structure can arise, however, as long as organisms have some ability to learn; in this way they can fill in the gaps in their innate ability with learned behaviour.

Turkel (1994) looks at a different aspect of the Baldwin Effect in order to explain the partially fixed, partially variable nature of UG. Assuming a principles and parameters model of this variation, he repeats Hinton and Nowlan's (1987) experiment and shows that a small shared set of variable parameters is the expected result of the learning-guided evolution of language. The three alleles of Hinton and Nowlan correspond in this case to either invariant principles (0 or 1) or flexible parameters (?). Each parameter can be switched to 0 or 1 during learning, so the principles are assumed to be in some sense pre-wired parameter settings. Two organisms are potential communicators if their genomes *match*, where matching is possible if a 0 on one genome corresponds to a 0 or ? on the other, and similarly a 1 corresponds to a 1 or ?. Learning in the simulation involves randomly switching the parameters of each organism in a pair of potential communicators. The fitness of the organisms is related to the number of random settings it takes for both organism's sets of parameters to match *exactly*.

The result of Turkel's simulation is that the population converges on a set of shared principles and a small number of shared parameters. Which particular loci on the genome become fixed as principles, which remain as parameters, and whether the principles are set to 0 or 1 are completely arbitrary and different from one run of the simulation to another. The proportion of remaining parameters, however, shows little variation from run to run.

Another approach to modelling the evolution of language is presented by Batali (1994) in an intriguing paper. Instead of relying on a rather abstract representation of principles and parameters, as in Turkel (1994), Batali considers the possibility that a general learning mechanism can evolve to incorporate innate biases to particular classes of language that it is presented with. Specifically, he evolves a population of recurrent neural networks (e.g. Elman 1990) given the task of learning simple context-free languages. Crucially, each network is given strings from a language with the same syntax, but with randomly chosen lexical items. The networks are thus unable to evolve to recognize exactly the language being presented.

Instead, the generations of networks gradually improve in their ability to learn the languages they are presented with by nativizing a disposition to learning *the particular class of languages in the simulation.*

The class of languages in the simulation can be described using a context-free grammar (although the author does not present it in this way):

$$S \rightarrow Push\ M^*\ Pop$$

$$M \rightarrow Idle^*\ (S)\ Idle^*$$

So, each sentence in the language class starts with a *Push*, ends with a *Pop*, has any number of *Idle*s, and any number of other *Push*es and *Pop*s as long as each *Push* on the left has a corresponding *Pop* on the right. The individual languages differed in the assignment of four possible lexical items (*a*, *b*, *c*, *d*) to the three categories. So, for example, *baadcadcdd* is a sentence in the language with the following assignment:

$$Push \rightarrow a$$
$$Push \rightarrow b$$
$$Pop \rightarrow d$$
$$Idle \rightarrow c$$

In order to parse a string in this class of languages, an automaton that knows the assignment of lexical items to categories must have some kind of counter. The counter will be incremented on encountering a *Push* and decremented at each *Pop*. Each *Idle* will not affect the counter. A valid string will return the counter to zero on encountering the last lexical item.

The networks in the simulation are each assigned a random language in this class and given the task of predicting when a sentence was finished (a good test of 'understanding' of the grammar without the need for supervised learning). The initial population of networks with random initial connections are fairly unsuccessful at this task after 500,000 characters of input. Selective breeding of networks on the basis of their final prediction ability is carried out so that the next generation has the *initial* connections of the best learners of the previous generation. Over (evolutionary) time, the performance of the networks improves markedly as the networks inherit an innate bias for learning this class of language. Specifically, the networks *learn* to associate *Push* and *Pop* symbols with an internal counter, and have an *innate* association of the zero value of this counter with the end-of-string prediction.

Batali's work is particularly fascinating as it suggests a way in which to marry connectionist accounts of language learning with generative accounts of language acquisition. By modelling the evolution of general-purpose learning machines, he has shown that there can be a gradual biologization of the common features of the multiple learning tasks that face a population, leaving specific features to be learnt. Just as we saw in Chapter 4 that language acquisition is a process of generalization over input data, evolution here is generalizing over learning problems. What remains to be explored is the extent of this kind of evolution's ability to generalize. If the distribution of input languages is constrained by functional pressures, what aspects of this distribution can the Baldwin Effect make innate?

Both Turkel's and Batali's simulations have their problems. For example, the particular settings of the innate principles in Turkel's evolutionary scenario are irrelevant to the fitness of the organisms—but how realistic is this? For Batali the most serious criticism could be that the actual languages that the networks learn are imposed by the experimenter rather than being generated by the organisms themselves, so how much can this tell us about the evolution of language? The value of these approaches, however, is in showing us that it is possible for natural selection to have shaped the human language faculty *partially to specify* the language we acquire. From looking at their results we can expect an innate LAD that evolved through natural selection to have some arbitrary constraints, but also to allow for variation.

In order for such models to solve the problem of the origin of specifically *functional* constraints as opposed to arbitrary ones, we would need to include functional pressures in the simulations. Batali's work shows that the broad design of the acquisition mechanism can become tailored to the problem of acquiring a class of languages, but this is far from the evolution of the particular constraints needed to rule out languages within this class that are harder to parse, for example. The Baldwin Effect shows us that gradual evolution of the LAD is possible, and that both arbitrary constraints and basic functional design features may become innate. It also shows us that there is a limit to this biologization, since the models of its effect predict that the set of occurring languages will never be completely specified innately (for further discussion, see e.g. Belew 1990; Christiansen 1994: §5.2.2; French and Messinger 1994).

Kirby and Hurford (1997*b*) and Briscoe (1997) take up the challenge of building processing pressures into evolutionary models. The models described in these papers specifically test how grammaticalization and biologization might interact, an approach to functionalism that has been termed *co-evolutionary linguistics* (see also Deacon 1997; Kirby 1998*a*; Hurford, in press; Hurford and Kirby, in press). As yet, this area of research is in its infancy and no clear conclusions can be drawn, but it seems clear that eventually a complete understanding of how function gives rise to universals must take both glossogenetic and phylogenetic adaptation into account. If this is true, then our understanding of language structure will have to integrate function and form, dynamical properties, and innateness.

6 Conclusion

The use to which language is put influences its form. In particular, the way that we process utterances is reflected in constraints on variation across languages. We can see this—as many functional–typologists have—by comparing processing asymmetries with cross-linguistic asymmetries. However, this is only the starting point for a complete explanation. It is important to tackle the *problem of linkage*, by making the connection between these asymmetries as explicit as possible.

I hope that, in its attempt to do so, this book has shown the value of looking at *how* processing pressures give rise to universals. The problem of linkage is challenging, because its solution touches on the subject matter of many different disciplines. I believe that a serious examination of the role of function in determining linguistic form forces us to view language as a dynamical, adaptive system—a system which we must look at from a holistic viewpoint if we are to hope to make adequate predictions about what universals are likely to emerge given particular functional pressures. Taking this viewpoint means taking into account the structure and influence not only of E-language and the mechanisms of its transmission, but also of I-language and the Chomskyan LAD.

The first central claim of this book is that:

Functional pressures influence linguistic selection, which operates locally in the cycle of acquisition and use, to give rise, globally, to observable language universals, over a historical timescale.

To illuminate this claim new universals have *not* been uncovered, although some novel interpretations of the cross-linguistic data on case-coding have been proposed. Similarly, a new psycholinguistic model has *not* been put forward, although the separation of m- and p-complexity may be considered as a contribution to this area. Instead, the link between these two halves of the explanation—the process of linguistic selection—has been made explicit. By doing so, simulations can be designed that allow us to test the implicit assumptions of functional typology.

In its acknowledgement of the central role of the dynamics of language use and acquisition, this book places a good deal of importance on language change. Although the simulations deal with the behaviour of individual speakers, we have taken a *macroscopic* view. In the study of universals we are essentially interested in the end result of all possible changes operating together; the relevant question being: is there a stable, emergent pattern cross-linguistically? In other words, individual changes in language and their causes are not our primary concern. Of course, the model of change should not be completely unrealistic or idealized. This is why it was considered important in Chapter 2 that the behaviour of the simulation matched the S-shaped curve observed by linguists interested in variation and change, as well as giving rise to the word-order types that we expect to find.

Another important result from Chapter 2 is the conclusion that the assumption of speaker altruism is not required in order to explain the fit of universals to parsing pressures. Instead, this fit is the inevitable result of the parser having a selective influence on the transmission of forms through the arena of use. This means that Newmeyer's (1991) innatist explanation is not the only possible one for the origin of universals that correspond to parsing pressures.

Chapter 3 poses the most serious challenge to any functional–typological view that simply assumes the link between processing and universals. The simulations show that hierarchical, or implicational, universals relating to relative clauses emerge *only* given competing functional pressures whose relative importance shifts over time. The stable, hierarchical universal is thus the result of a complex, unstable push–pull between speaker and hearer. A 'type-graph' formalism suggested by Greenberg (1978) is used to help understand this result, although here it is clear that the simulation method itself is invaluable in testing the behaviour of the complex adaptive systems model. The separation of two competing types of complexity in this chapter also suggests a reassessment of the case-coding distinction for relative clauses. The skewing, cross-linguistically, of various types of relative clause on the hierarchy is predicted on the basis of the relative morphological complexity of the strategy for forming each type. This seems to fit the available data rather well, although a larger-scale typological survey is required.

Up to this point, the type of explanation examined relies solely on features of the arena of use (i.e. processing operating to select variant forms). However, an important finding of this book is that this type of functional explanation is incomplete without a consideration of the role of innate constraints on variation. My second central claim is therefore that:

Adaptation by linguistic selection operates within constraints imposed by Universal Grammar.

This is demonstrated in Chapter 4, where some features of innate UG act to limit and affect the adaptive process in interesting ways. It is only with a careful examination of these 'environmental' constraints imposed by our innate faculty that functionalist explanations can be saved from explanatory inadequacy (e.g. in the link between processing and relative clauses). It also helps us to understand puzzling features of individual languages (such as animacy effects) as having their roots in apparently unrelated processing pressures.

To some, the marriage of the functionalist approach and Chomskyan nativism may seem inappropriate. The assumption of the autonomy of syntax is at the core of the generative programme, and admitting language processing as a factor in the origin of linguistic structure appears to undermine this assumption. In Chapter 5 this belief is attacked on two levels. First, it is clear that the simulations of variation and change put forward here are quite compatible with the autonomy thesis. Secondly, a review of some of the recent literature on evolution admits the possibility of a functional underpinning for the autonomous syntactic principles themselves. This leads to a third claim (which mirrors our first two in interesting ways):

Functional pressures influence natural selection, which operates within physical and embryological constraints to give rise to an autonomous LAD, or UG, over a biological timescale.

Perhaps because research on human evolution is still at a preliminary stage, this chapter has raised many unanswered questions. We are left with a complex picture of the multiple interactions of function, innateness, and selection that we are only beginning to understand. After examining these interactions in terms of the link between processing and universals, however, I believe we can now at least ask the *right* questions.

Finally, the most important message of this book is that the problem of explaining universals goes to the very heart of most areas of modern linguistics. If we are to understand these emergent properties of language, we need a more eclectic approach than is apparent in much of the literature. Whilst researchers continue to place themselves solely in the 'functionalist' camp or the 'formalist' camp, we can hope to see only half of the picture.

References

Ackley, David, and Littman, Michael (1991), 'Interactions between Learning and Evolution', in C. G. Langton, C. Taylor, J. D. Farmer, and S. Ramussen (eds.), *Artificial Life II* (Reading, Mass.: Addison-Wesley), 487–509.

——— ——— (1994), 'Altruism in the Evolution of Communication', in Rodney Brooks and Pattie Maes (eds.), *Artificial Life IV* (Cambridge, Mass.: MIT Press), 40–8.

Andersen, Henning (1972), 'Diphthongization', *Language*, 48: 11–50.

——— (1973), 'Abductive and Deductive Change', *Language*, 40: 765–93.

Bakker, Dik (1994), *Formal and Computational Aspects of Functional Grammar and Language Typology* (Dordrecht: Foris).

Baldwin, J. M. (1896), 'A New Factor in Evolution', *American Naturalist*, 30: 441–51.

Batali, John (1994), 'Innate Biases and Critical Periods: Combining Evolution and Learning in the Acquisition of Syntax', in Rodney Brooks and Pattie Maes (eds.), *Artificial Life IV* (Cambridge, Mass.: MIT Press), 160–71.

——— (1998), 'Computational Simulations of the Emergence of Grammar', in James Hurford, Michael Studdert-Kennedy, and Chris Knight (eds.), *Approaches to the Evolution of Language: Social and Cognitive Bases* (Cambridge: Cambridge University Press), 405–26.

Belew, Richard (1990), 'Evolution, Learning, and Culture: Computational Metaphors for Adaptive Algorithms', *Complex Systems*, 4: 11–49.

Berwick, R. C., and Weinberg, A. S. (1984), *The Grammatical Basis of Linguistic Performance: Language Use and Acquisition* (Cambridge, Mass.: MIT Press).

Bickerton, Derek (1990), *Language and Species* (Chicago: University of Chicago Press).

Briscoe, Ted (1997), 'Language Acquisition: The Bioprogram Hypothesis and the Baldwin Effect', MS, Computer Laboratory, University of Cambridge.

Bybee, Joan (1985), *Morphology: A Study in the Relation between Meaning and Form* (Amsterdam: John Benjamins).

——— (1988), 'The Diachronic Dimension in Explanation', in John A. Hawkins (ed.), *Explaining Language Universals* (Oxford: Blackwell).

Cangelosi, Angelo, and Parisi, Domenico (1996), 'The Emergence of a Language in an Evolving Population of Neural Networks', Technical Report NSAL-96004, National Research Council, Rome.

Cann, Ronnie, and Tait, Mary (1990), 'Free Relatives Revisited', MS, University of Edinburgh.

Chomsky, Noam (1964), *Current Issues in Linguistic Theory* (The Hague: Mouton).

——— (1975), 'Questions of Form and Interpretation', *Linguistic Analysis*, 1: 75–109.

——— (1980), *Rules and Representations* (New York: Columbia University Press).

——— (1981), *Lectures on Government and Binding* (Dordrecht: Foris).

——— (1986), *Knowledge of Language* (New York: Praeger).

Chomsky, Noam (1988), *Language and Problems of Knowledge: The Managua Lectures* (Cambridge, Mass.: MIT Press).

—— (1993), 'A Minimalist Program for Linguistic Theory', in K. Hale and S. J. Keyser (eds.), *The View from Building 20* (Cambridge, Mass.: MIT Press), 1–52.

—— and Lasnik, H. (1977), 'Filters and Control', *Linguistic Inquiry*, 8: 425–504.

Christiansen, Morten (1994), 'Infinite Languages, Finite Minds: Connectionism, Learning and Linguistic Structure', dissertation, University of Edinburgh.

Clancy, Patricia, Lee, Hyeonijin, and Zoh, Myeong-Han (1986), 'Processing Strategies in the Acquisition of Relative Clauses: Universal Principles and Language-Specific Realizations', *Cognition*, 24: 225–62.

Clark, Robert (1996), 'Internal and External Factors Affecting Language Change: A Computational Model', Master's thesis, University of Edinburgh.

Clark, Robin, and Roberts, Ian (1993), 'A Computational Model of Language Learnability and Language Change', *Linguistic Inquiry*, 24: 299–345.

Comrie, Bernard (1981), *Language Universals and Linguistic Typology* (Oxford: Blackwell).

—— and Keenan, Edward (1979), 'Noun Phrase Accessibility Revisited', *Language*, 55: 649–64.

Corbett, Greville (1983), *Hierarchies, Targets and Controllers: Agreement Patterns in Slavic* (London: Croom Helm).

Croft, William (1990), *Typology and Universals* (Cambridge: Cambridge University Press).

—— (1993), 'Functional-Typological Theory in its Historical and Intellectual Context', *Sprachtypologie und Universalienforschung*, 46: 15–26.

Cutler, A., Hawkins, J., and Gilligan, G. (1985), 'The Suffixing Preference: A Processing Explanation', *Linguistics*, 23: 723–58.

Cziko, Gary (1995), *Without Miracles: Universal Selection Theory and the Second Darwinian Revolution* (Cambridge, Mass.: MIT Press).

Dawkins, Richard (1982), *The Extended Phenotype* (Oxford: Freeman).

Deacon, Terrence W. (1997), *The Symbolic Species: The Co-Evolution of Language and the Brain* (New York: Norton).

DeVilliers, J. G., Tager-Flusberg, H. B., Hakuta, K., and Cohen, M. (1979), 'Children's Comprehension of Relative Clauses', *Journal of Psycholinguistic Research*, 8: 499–518.

Dryer, Matthew (1980), 'The Positional Tendencies of Sentential Noun Phrases in Universal Grammar', *Canadian Journal of Linguistics*, 25: 123–95.

—— (1991), 'SVO Languages and the OV:VO Typology', *Journal of Linguistics*, 27: 443–82.

—— (1992), 'The Greenbergian Word Order Correlations', *Language*, 68: 81–138.

DuBois, John (1987), 'The Discourse Basis of Ergativity', *Language*, 64: 805–55.

Elman, Jeffrey (1990), 'Finding Structure in Time', *Cognitive Science*, 14: 179–211.

—— (1991), 'Incremental Learning, or the Importance of Starting Small', in *Program of the 13th Annual Conference of the Cognitive Science Society*, (Hillsdale, NJ: Cognitive Science Society, Lawrence Erlbaum), 443–8.

Fay, D. (1980), 'Transformational Errors', in V. A. Fromkin (ed.), *Errors in Linguistic Performance: Slips of the Tongue, Ear, Pen and Hand* (New York: Academic Press), 111–12.

Fischer, O. (1992), 'Syntax', in N. Blake (ed.), *The Cambridge History of the English Language, ii. 1066–1476* (Cambridge: Cambridge University Press), 207–408.

Fodor, Jerry A. (1983), *The Modularity of Mind* (Cambridge, Mass.: MIT Press).

Frazier, L. (1985), 'Syntactic Complexity', in D. Dowty, L. Karttunen, and A. Zwicky (eds.), *Natural Language Parsing: Psychological, Computational, and Theoretical Perspectives* (Cambridge: Cambridge University Press).

—— and Rayner, K. (1988), 'Parameterizing the Language Processing System: Left vs. Right Branching within and across Languages', in J. A. Hawkins (ed.), *Explaining Language Universals* (Oxford: Blackwell).

French, Robert, and Messinger, Adam (1994), 'Genes, Phenes and the Baldwin Effect: Learning and Evolution in a Simulated Population', in Rodney Brooks and Pattie Maes (eds.), *Artificial Life IV* (Cambridge, Mass.: MIT Press), 277–82.

Gell-Mann, Murray (1992), 'Complexity and Complex Adaptive Systems', in J. A. Hawkins and M. Gell-Mann (eds.), *The Evolution of Human Languages* (Reading Mass.: Addison-Wesley), 3–18.

Giorgi, Alessandra, and Longobardi, Giuseppe (1991), *The Syntax of Noun Phrases: Configuration, Parameters and Empty Categories* (Cambridge: Cambridge University Press).

Givón, Talmy (1979), *On Understanding Grammar* (New York: Academic Press).

—— (1985), 'Iconicity, Isomorphism and Non-Arbitrary Coding in Syntax,' in John Haiman (ed.), *Iconocity in Syntax* (Amsterdam: John Benjamins), 187–220.

Gould, Stephen J. (1983), *Hens' Teeth and Horses' Toes* (Harmondsworth: Penguin).

—— and Lewontin, R. C. (1979), 'The Spandrels of San Marco and the Panglossian Paradigm: A Critique of the Adaptationist Programme', *Proceedings of the Royal Society of London*, 205: 281–8.

—— and Vrba, E. S. (1982), 'Exaptation — a Missing Term in the Science of Form', *Paleobiology*, 8: 4–15.

Greenberg, Joseph (1963), 'Some Universals of Grammar with Particular Reference to the Order of Meaningful Elements', in Joseph Greenberg (ed.), *Universals of Language* (Cambridge, Mass.: MIT Press), 73–113.

—— (1966), *Language Universals with Special Reference to Feature Hierarchies* (The Hague: Mouton).

—— (1978), 'Diachrony, Synchrony, and Language Universals', in Joseph Greenberg (ed.), *Universals of Human Language 1, Method and Theory* (Stanford, Calif.: Stanford University Press), 61–91.

Grimm, H., Scholer H., and Wintermantel, M. (1975), *Zur Entwicklung sprachlicher Strukturformen bei Kindern* (Beltz).

Grimshaw, J. (1997), 'Projection, Heads and Optimality', *Linguistic Inquiry*, 28: 373–422.

Groos, A., and Riemsdijk, H. van (1979), 'Matching Effects in Free Relatives: A Parameter of Core Grammar', in A. Belletti, L. Brandi, and L. Rizzi (eds.), *Theory of Markedness in Generative Grammar* (Pisa: Scuola Normale Superiore), 171–216.

Haegeman, Liliane (1991), *Introduction to Government and Binding Theory* (Oxford: Blackwell).

Haiman, John (1985), *Natural Syntax: Iconicity and Erosion* (Cambridge: Cambridge University Press).

Hall, Christopher (1988), 'Integrating Diachronic and Processing Principles in Explaining the Suffixing Preference', in John A. Hawkins (ed.), *Explaining Language Universals* (Oxford: Blackwell), 321–49.

—— (1992), *Morphology and Mind: A Unified Approach to Explanation in Linguistics* (London: Routledge).

Hawkins, John A. (1983), *Word Order Universals* (New York: Academic Press).

—— (1988), 'Explaining Language Universals', in John A. Hawkins (ed.), *Explaining Language Universals* (Oxford: Blackwell), 3–28.

—— (1990), 'A Parsing Theory of Word Order Universals', *Linguistic Inquiry*, 21: 223–61.

—— (1992*a*), 'Innateness and Function in Language Universals', in J. A. Hawkins, and M. Gell-Mann (eds.), *The Evolution of Human Languages* (Reading, Mass.: Addison-Wesley).

—— (1992*b*), 'Syntactic Weight versus Information Structure in Word Order Variation', in J. Jacobs (ed.), *Special Issue No. 4*, (Informationsstruktur und Grammatik, Linguistische Berichte), 196–219.

—— (1993), 'Heads, Parsing, and Word Order Universals', in Greville G. Corbett, Norman M. Fraser, and Scott McGlashan (eds.), *Heads in Grammatical Theory*, (Cambridge: Cambridge University Press), 231–65.

—— (1994*a*), *A Performance Theory of Order and Constituency* (Cambridge: Cambridge University Press).

—— (1994*b*), 'Some Issues in a Performance Theory of Word Order', MS, University of Southern California.

Hawkins, R. (1981), 'Towards an Account of the Possessive Constructions *np's n* and *the n of np*', *Journal of Linguistics*, 17: 247–69.

Heine, Bernd, Claudi, Ulrike, and Hunnemeyer, Friederike (1991), *Grammaticalization: A Conceptual Framework* (Chicago: University of Chicago Press).

Hinton, G., and Nowlan, S. (1987), 'How Learning can Guide Evolution', *Complex Systems*, 1: 495–502.

Hoekstra, Teun, and Kooij, Jan G. (1988), 'The Innateness Hypothesis', in John A. Hawkins (ed.), *Explaining Language Universals* (Oxford: Blackwell), 31–55.

Huddleston, R. (1984), *Introduction to the Grammar of English* (Cambridge: Cambridge University Press).

Hurford, James (1987), *Language and Number: The Emergence of a Cognitive System* (Cambridge, Mass.: Blackwell).

—— (1989), 'Biological Evolution of the Saussurean Sign as a Component of the Language Acquisition Device', *Lingua*, 77: 187–222.

—— (1990), 'Nativist and Functional Explanations in Language Acquisition', in I. M. Roca (ed.), *Logical Issues in Language Acquisition* (Dordrecht: Foris), 85–136.

—— (1991), 'The Evolution of the Critical Period for Language Acquisition', *Cognition*, 40: 159–201.

—— (in press), 'The Evolution of Language and Languages', in Chris Knight, Robin Dunbar, and Camilla Power (eds.), *The Evolution of Culture* (Edinburgh: Edinburgh University Press).

—— and Kirby, Simon (1995), 'Neural Preconditions for Proto-Language', *Behavioural and Brain Sciences*, 18: 193–4.

—— —— (in press), 'Co-Evolution of Language-Size and the Critical Period', in David Birdsong (ed.), *New Perspectives on the Critical Period Hypothesis and Second Language Acquisition* (Mahwah, NJ: Lawrence Erlbaum).

Hyman, L. (1984), 'Form and Substance in Language Universals', in B. Butterworth, B. Comrie, and O. Dahl (eds.), *Explanations for Language Universals* (The Hague: Mouton), 67–85.

Jackendoff, R. (1977), *X-Syntax: A Study of Phrase Structure* (Cambridge, Mass.: MIT Press).

Kail, M. (1975), 'Étude génétique de la reproduction de phrases relatives: 1. reproduction immédiate', *L'Année psychologique*, 75: 109–26.

Keenan, Edward (1972a), 'The Logical Status of Deep Structures', in L. Heilmann (ed.), *Proceedings of the Eleventh International Congress of Linguists* (Bologna: Societa editrice il Mulino).

—— (1972b), 'Relative Clause Formation in Malagasy', in Paul Peranteau, Judith Levi, and Gloria Phares (eds.), *The Chicago Which Hunt* (Chicago: Chicago Linguistics Society), 169–89.

—— and Comrie, Bernard (1977), 'Noun Phrase Accessibility and Universal Grammar', *Linguistic Inquiry*, 8: 63–99.

—— and Hawkins, Sarah (1987), 'The Psychological Validity of the Accessibility Hierarchy', in Edward Keenan (ed.), *Universal Grammar: 15 Essays* (London: Croom Helm), 60–85.

Keller, Rudi (1994), *On Language Change: The Invisible Hand in Language* (London: Routledge).

Kirby, Simon (1994a), 'Adaptive Explanations for Language Universals: A Model of Hawkins' Performance Theory', *Sprachtypologie und Universalienforschung*, 47: 186–210.

—— (1997), 'Competing Motivations and Emergence: Explaining Implicational Hierarchies', *Language Typology*, 1: 5–31.

—— (1998a), 'Fitness and the Selective Adaptation of Language', in J. Hurford, M. Studdert-Kennedy, and C. Knight (eds.), *Approaches to the Evolution of Language: Social and Cognitive Bases* (Cambridge: Cambridge University Press), 359–83.

—— (1998b), 'Constraints on Constraints, or the Limits of Functional Adaptation', in M. Noonan, E. Moravscik, and F. Newmeyer (eds.), *Functionalism/Formalism: Acquisition and Diachrony* (Amsterdam: John Benjamins).

—— (1998c), 'Language Evolution without Natural Selection: From Vocabulary to Syntax in a Population of Learners', Technical Report EOPL-98-1, Department of Linguistics, University of Edinburgh.

—— and Hurford, James (1997a), 'The Evolution of Incremental Learning: Language, Development and Critical Periods', Occasional Paper EOPL-97-2, Department of Linguistics, University of Edinburgh.

Kirby, Simon, and Hurford, James (1997*b*), 'Learning, Culture and Evolution in the Origin of Linguistic Constraints', in Phil Husbands and Inman Harvey (eds.), *Fourth European Conference on Artificial Life* (Cambridge, Mass.: MIT Press), 493–502.

Kroch, Anthony (1989*a*), 'Function and Grammar in the History of English', in Ralph Fasold, and Deborah Schiffrin (eds.), *Language Change and Variation*, (Amsterdam: John Benjamins), 133–72.

—— (1989*b*), 'Reflexes of Grammar in Patterns of Language Change', *Language Variation and Change*, 1: 199–244.

—— (1994), 'Morphosyntactic Variation', in K. Beals (ed.), *Papers from the 30th Regional Meeting of the Chicago Linguistics Society* (Chicago: Chicago Linguistics Society).

Labov, W. (1972), *Sociolinguistic Patterns* (Philadelphia, Pa.: University of Pennsylvania Press).

Lass, Roger (1980), *On Explaining Language Change* (Cambridge: Cambridge University Press).

Levelt, Willem (1983), 'Monitoring and Self-Repair in Speech', *Cognition*, 14: 41–104.

—— (1989), *Speaking: From Intention to Articulation* (Cambridge, Mass.: MIT Press).

Lewontin, R. (1974), *The Genetic Basis of Evolutionary Change* (New York: Columbia University Press).

Li, C., and Thompson, S. (1975), 'The Semantic Function of Word Order: A Case Study in Mandarin', in C. Li (ed.), *Word Order and Word Order Change* (Austin, Tex.: University of Texas Press).

Lightfoot, David (1989), 'The Child's Trigger Experience: Degree-0 Learnability', *Behavioural and Brain Sciences*, 12: 321–34.

—— (1991), 'Subjacency and Sex', *Language and Communication*, 11: 3–28.

MacLennan, Bruce (1991), 'Synthetic Ethology: An Approach to the Study of Communication', in C. G. Langton, C. Taylor, J. D. Farmer, and S. Ramussen (eds.), *Artificial Life II* (Reading, Mass.: Addison-Wesley), 631–57.

—— and Burghardt, Gordon M. (1993), 'Synthetic Ethology and the Evolution of Cooperative Communication', *Adaptive Behaviour*, 2: 161–87.

MacWhinney, B. (1982), 'Basic Syntactic Processes', in S. Kuczaj (ed.), *Language Acquisition: i. Syntax and Semantics* (Mahwah, NJ: Lawrence Erlbaum).

—— and Pleh, C. (1988), 'The Processing of Restrictive Relative Clauses in Hungarian', *Cognition*, 29: 95–141.

Manzini, R., and Wexler, K. (1987), 'Parameters, Binding Theory and Learnability', *Linguistic Inquiry*, 18: 413–44.

Marantz, Alec (1995), 'The Minimalist Program', in Gert Webelhuth (ed.), *Government and Binding Theory and the Minimalist Program* (Oxford: Blackwell), 348–82.

Marcus, Mitchell P. (1980), *A Theory of Syntactic Recognition for Natural Language* (Cambridge, Mass.: MIT Press).

Maxwell, Daniel (1979), 'Strategies of Relativization and NP Accessibility', *Language*, 55: 352–71.

Mayr, E. (1982), *The Growth of Biological Thought* (Cambridge, Mass.: Harvard University Press).

McGill, Steven (1993), 'Linguistic Evolution: Language Change, Variation and Selection', MS, University of Edinburgh.

Morolong, M., and Hyman, L. H. (1977), 'Animacy, Objects and Clitics in Sesotho', *Studies in African Linguistics*, 8: 199–218.

Newmeyer, Frederick J. (1991), 'Functional Explanation in Linguistics and the Origins of Language', *Language and Communication*, 11: 3–28.

—— (1992), 'Iconicity and Generative Grammar', *Language*, 68: 756–96.

—— (1994*a*), 'Competing Motivations and Synchronic Analysis', *Sprachtypologie und Universalienforschung*, 47: 67–77.

—— (1994*b*), 'A note on Chomsky on Form and Function', *Journal of Linguistics*, 30: 245–51.

—— (1998), *Language Form and Language Function* (Cambridge, Mass.: MIT Press).

Niyogi, Partha, and Berwick, Robert (1995), 'The Logical Problem of Language Change', Technical Report AI Memo 1516/CBCL Paper 115, MIT AI Laboratory and Center for Biological and Computational Learning, Department of Brain and Cognitive Sciences.

Nolfi, Stefano, Elman, Jeffrey, and Parisi, Domenico (1994), 'Learning and Evolution in Neural Networks', *Adaptive Behaviour*, 3: 5–28.

Oliphant, Michael (1996), 'The Dilemma of Saussurean Communication', *BioSystems*, 37: 31–8.

—— (1997), 'Formal Approaches to Innate and Learned Communication: Laying the Foundation for Language', dissertation, University of California at San Diego.

—— and Batali, John, (1996), 'Learning and the Emergence of Coordinated Communication', Draft MS.

Panov, M. V. (1968) (ed.), *Russkij jazyk i socetskoe obščestvo, III, Morfologija i sintaksis sovremennogo russkogo jazyka* (Moscow: Nauka).

Piattelli-Palmerini, M. (1989), 'Evolution, Selection and Cognition: From "Learning" to Parameter Setting in Biology and the Study of Language', *Cognition*, 31: 1–44.

Pinker, Steven, and Bloom, Paul (1990), 'Natural Language and Natural Selection', *Behavioral and Brain Sciences*, 13: 707–84.

Pollard, Carl, and Sag, Ivan (1994), *Head-Driven Phrase Structure Grammar* (Chicago: University of Chicago Press).

Rickford, John, Wasow, Thomas, Mendoza-Denton, Norma, and Espinoza, Juli (1995), 'Syntactic Variation and Change in Progress: Loss of Verbal Coda in Topic-Restricting *as far as* Constructions', *Language*, 71: 102–31.

Riemsdijk, H. van, and Williams, E. (1986), *Introduction to the Theory of Grammar* (Cambridge, Mass.: MIT Press).

Sheldon, Amy (1974), 'On the Role of Parallel Function in the Acquisition of Relative Clauses in English', *Journal of Verbal Learning and Verbal Behaviour*, 13: 272–81.

—— (1977), 'The Acquisition of Relative Clauses in French and English: Implications for Language-Learning Universals', in F. Eckman (ed.), *Current Themes in Linguistics* (Washington: Hemisphere).

Shibatani, Masayoshi (1990), *The Languages of Japan* (Cambridge: Cambridge University Press).

Sober, Elliot (1984), *The Nature of Selection: Evolutionary Theory in Philosophical Focus* (Cambridge, Mass.: MIT Press).

Sperber, D., and Wilson, D. (1986), *Relevance: Communication and Cognition* (Oxford: Blackwell).

Spiess, Eliot (1989), *Genes in Populations* (New York: John Wiley & Sons).

Steels, Luc (1996), 'Emergent Adaptive Lexicons', in P. Maes (ed.), *Proceedings of the Simulation of Adaptive Behavior Conference* (Cambridge, Mass.: MIT Press).

—— (1997), 'The Synthetic Modelling of Language Origins', *Evolution of Communication*, 1: 1–34.

Stowell, T. (1981), 'Origins of Phrase Structure', dissertation, MIT.

Tallerman, Maggie (1990), 'Relativisation Strategies: NP Accessibility in Welsh', *Journal of Linguistics*, 26: 291–314.

Tavakolian, S. (1981), 'The Conjoined-Clause Analysis of Relative Clauses', in S. Tavakolian (ed.), *Language Acquisition and Linguistic Theory* (Cambridge, Mass.: MIT Press), 167–87.

Tiersma, Peter (1982), 'Local and General Markedness', *Language*, 58: 832–49.

Traugott, Elizabeth C. and Heine, Bernd (1991), *Approaches to Grammaticalization, i* (Amsterdam: John Benjamins).

Travis, L. (1984), 'Parameters and Effects of Word Order Variation', dissertation, MIT.

Turkel, William (1994), 'The Learning-Guided Evolution of Natural Language', MS, University of British Columbia.

Vanek, A. L. (1977), 'Aspects of Subject–Verb Agreement', *Current Inquiry into Language and Linguistics*, 23.

Wedgwood, Daniel (1995), 'Grammaticalisation by Re-analysis in an Adaptive Model of Language Change: A Case Study of the English Genitive Constructions', Master's thesis, University of Edinburgh.

Werner, Gregory, and Dyer, Michael (1991), 'Evolution of Communication in Artificial Organisms', in C. G. Langton, C. Taylor, J. D. Farmer, and S. Ramussen (eds.), *Artificial Life II* (Reading, Mass.: Addison-Wesley), 659–87.

Wilkins, Wendy, and Wakefield, Jennie (1995), 'Brain Evolution and Neurolinguistic Preconditions', *Behavioral and Brain Sciences*, 18: 161–226.

Witkowski, Stanley R., and Brown, Cecil H. (1983), 'Marking-Reversals and Cultural Importance', *Language*, 59: 569–82.

Index

Please note that page numbers in bold type indicate a reference to a Figure.